NO THANKS

Jessica,
Enjoy the read and
live your life with
joy!!
—Keturah Kendrick

NO THANKS

Black, Female, and Living in the Martyr-Free Zone

Keturah Kendrick

SHE WRITES PRESS

Published 2019
Printed in the United States of America
ISBN: 978-1-63152-535-3 pbk
ISBN: 978-1-63152-536-0 ebk
Library of Congress Control Number: 2018966933

For information, address:
She Writes Press
1569 Solano Ave #546
Berkeley, CA 94707

She Writes Press is a division of SparkPoint Studio, LLC.

Book design by Stacey Aaronson

NO
THANKS

CONTENTS

Preface

———

I wrote this book because twenty years ago I needed to read it. I was not aware that I needed the words within these pages so I did not go in search of them. There is a chance that what I have penned here has been written on numerous occasions by numerous women like me. Nevertheless, I must submit this work as documentation.

Somewhere, I am certain, there is a young black woman curled up on a couch with a man she adores. This man has offered her his sperm and his last name. She wants to be as excited about this offer as he is. She wants to tell him she does want to marry him, but not right now. Maybe in a few years, when she feels ready. She hasn't said this to him because it doesn't feel like the truth.

Somewhere, I know, there is a black girl sitting on the floor of her studio apartment. She hasn't replied to the email from her soror urging, *Send me your resume. I can get you an interview for a position it takes most people years after graduation to be considered for.* This black girl started her research during her final semester. A year later, she has done all the calculations. Thought about the obstacles and how they can be overcome. If she teaches English abroad for three to six years, she can pay off her student loans, travel to several parts of the world, and invest in a modest condo that she can sell off for a healthy profit if she chooses to return to the United States.

Somewhere, there is a black millennial who has stopped going to church because she no longer wants to pretend she is a believer. She was respectful of her parents' belief the entire time she lived under their roof. She knew better than to express doubt in their god and irritation with the men who ran his church. Now that she is an adult, there is no longer a need for pretense.

Each of these black women thinks she is strange. She questions her reasoning and silences the thoughts that could mean she is insane. This is not what she should want. This is not how she should embark on black womanhood. She will make her choices regardless. The woman in love will not marry her good black man, nor will she birth and raise children. The college graduate will thank her soror for looking out for her before buying a one-way ticket to Thailand. The atheist will ignore her community's prayers for her soul as she lives her life free of a desire for salvation.

But there will be this feeling they cannot shake: *Something is not quite right about me.* They won't understand why their decisions about their lives cause so many whispers, invite unsolicited advice, and spark concern for their futures. And this quiet chastisement by their community will cause them to question their choices. Eventually, with enough reminders that they are unicorns, they will follow orders and try to chip away at the weird horn protruding from their foreheads.

It is with this book that I say to these women: Sis, you are not crazy. Neither are you alone.

1

For Clarity's Sake

1.

*L*et's begin with what freedom is not.

I don't seek a life in which I am connected to no one and no one is connected to me. I rejoice in the privilege of sharing this earthly space with those who uplift me, and even those who annoy me. I am committed to the well-being of my fellow humans, even though it is troublesome. I devote myself to the happiness of the people with whom I share this earth even though it requires much from me.

I don't want to be alone. I am much too extroverted. My heart's too big. I like to talk too much. I derive too much pleasure from engaging with people to propose that my emancipation is the metaphorical equivalent of a misguided monk sealing himself in a cave as he awaits Nirvana. If my entrance into enlightenment requires my exit from humanity, I choose this place we call present-day reality.

Freedom does not mean releasing oneself from any and all expectations.

To define freedom is not to write a treatise for the cowardly, the disconnected, the indifferent, and then declare such a document your well-earned escape.

We who believe in freedom also believe in people.

Ella Baker said, "We who believe in freedom will not rest until it comes." But if we are to have the unrestricted movement to fight for the liberation of others, we must declare it for ourselves first.

2.

I COULD SHARE MY OWN STORY OF PUSHING BACK against the expectation that I exist solely in relation to my obligation to care for family. However, I have met so many other black women over the years whose journeys mirror my own. Women with stories of rejecting the notion that their choices must always consider the needs of others. One of these women is my good friend, Grace.

When Grace was twenty-three, she came home for a family reunion. She had graduated from college a year earlier and still had not made it back home to allow the elders in the family to fawn over her, to point to her as an example for younger cousins to emulate. She was looking forward to the moment when the old folk were out of earshot so she could "sell" college to her bored cousins in ways they would want to hear.

The chance to reconnect with family was coming at just the right time. A southerner by birth, when it came to selecting a school, Grace had made the safest choice for a lower-middle-class black girl whose parents had never left the town where they were born. She chose a college that was out of that town, but still in the South. Close enough for her mother to feel she was more or less home, yet far enough away for Grace to begin her calculated escape from the suffocation of small-town life to the exhilaration of a big city.

Grace's mother had figured out what she was doing. Her daughter had been planning to call some other place home from the moment she announced she would be going to a college a four-hour drive away from her hometown. After graduation, she never even looked for a job in the city closest to the small town where her family lived. She didn't respond to her mother's hints about the eligible men who were buying houses with the income from their stable jobs only an hour away from where Grace had dirtied up her church clothes chasing after cousins in the backyard. Instead, Grace announced a move even farther away. And this move was not prompted by the acquisition of any tangible thing. Not only had she not found funding for a graduate school program, she had not even applied to any such program. She did not even have a good job already lined up in this new place.

While the rest of the family gossiped about the people who were absent from the reunion, Grace's mother and aunts took her aside. "Are you forgetting you have a mother? That she needs you?" Her mother's elder sister seemed offended that her niece had not even considered moving back home once she was done with her education.

Grace felt ambushed and confused. Her mother was not dying from an incurable disease; nor was she old and infirm—an invalid whose Social Security check would not stretch far enough to get her through her golden years.

"What are you talking about?" she asked. "What does she need me for?"

The aunts were vague. Grace's mother was not. "I feel like if you would just come home, if you would just come back to be with us, everyone would be happier. I would be happier."

How does an adult daughter respond to the suggestion that her life choices are tied to her mother's happiness? Grace didn't respond. She just moved.

For years, her visits back home were strained by her mother's frequent reminders that she had chosen New York City over her family. Things were tense.

Here is what Grace and I both free ourselves from: the people who love us expecting us to contort ourselves into shapes that fit more neatly into their lives. Yes, Grace's mother is an extreme version of what many families ask women to do all the time while pretending they are not asking us to do it in the first place. The demands made of Grace personify the expectations families place on the shoulders of girl children all around the world.

We will not chain ourselves to your expectations for us. You will not be allowed to direct our performance of daughter, sister, cousin, auntie, [insert any other role women are assigned that requires tending to some other person that is not herself].

Mothers. Fathers. Sisters. Brothers. Cousins. Uncles. Aunties. Playcousins. Playsisters. Playuncles. None are entitled to the blueprints of my life. None will be given the deed to my choices and allowed to edit them in ways that make the terms more amenable to their tastes.

Grace and I, on behalf of the women who have not yet

proclaimed their freedom, would like it to be known that we will not be held accountable to the conditions and guidelines our families and communities decide are the best way for us to fulfill our responsibilities as members of the tribe. No one ever says the word "prison," but it is an accurate description nonetheless. Barbed wire is wrapped around your throat as the people who love you whisper, "You need this just as much as I do."

3.

SINGLE, HETEROSEXUAL MEN INTRIGUE ME. THOSE who believe that their singleness, straightness *and* ability to conduct themselves as adults should make them extraordinary in the eyes of single women fascinate me. Brenda, a close acquaintance, briefly dated one such heterosexual male. Years later, she is still awed at what those handful of dates taught her about the perception of black women who still choose themselves when given the option of a heterosexual male who is able to stand upright and blink simultaneously.

Michael mentioned his child to Brenda on their third date. "My son has managed to inherit my most annoying traits. It is maddening to argue with yourself." Michael engaged in a hearty laugh that slowed when Brenda's face reflected hesitancy instead of amusement.

"You have a son?" She retraced in her mind the exact number of times they had met somewhere to eat and/or go to a movie. Yup, it had been exactly two times before this one.

"Well, yes."

"It took you a long time to tell me that." Brenda tried to

taper her voice so it didn't sound accusatory. This was difficult to do, because she *was* accusing Michael of something: withholding from her that he was someone's father.

"I wouldn't really say that." He sat up straighter in his chair, thrown off by Brenda's reaction to the nonchalant mention of his child. "It just never came up before."

Brenda still did not chuckle at his anecdote. She didn't ask how old his son was or what kind of antics he got into. She noticed Michael noticing her inability to mask her irritation with his omitting a key piece of information—one that, she felt, a potential mate would tend to reveal on the first date.

"I don't know why you look annoyed." Unlike Brenda, Michael made no effort to take the accusation out of his voice. "Most women would be happy to meet a man who is devoted to his child and has a good relationship with him."

Brenda decided there would not be a fourth date. When she told Michael she did not think they were a good fit, he implied that she had not given him a fair chance. As he explained that women sometimes took men's stupid comments too seriously, Brenda replayed the sentence he had said to her several times in her mind.

Most women . . .

Most women would be happy . . .

Most women would be happy to meet a man . . .

By the third replay, she had heard what Michael was really saying, though he was smart enough not to have allowed the words to fall from his lips.

You are a strange woman to find an issue with my not leading with the fact that I'm a single father so you could make an

informed decision about whether or not you wanted to be in-
volved with me and my son and his mother.

And while Michael now tried to convince her that she
was unaware of the mistake she was making by not pursuing
courtship with him, Brenda found it hard not to burst into
laughter. Perhaps, if it were still the twentieth century,
Michael would have just said:

You are one of those uppity black women who is all about
what you want and what you need and cannot be grateful that
you have met a good black man who actually wants to date you
and here you are, not laughing at the joke he made about his son
that proves he is an active and engaged father.

When Brenda told me this story, she rolled her eyes as if
to reiterate how irritated she still was years later. "During
that period," she said, "I wasn't sure if I wanted the disrup-
tion in my life that children bring, but I was clear I preferred
to date men who had not already started families with other
women. What really agitated me, though, was his condescension. His tone implied that since I was no longer in my twenties and was now dating with a purpose, I was ridiculous for
having boundaries or preferences that kept my best interest
in mind."

I have had versions of Michael sit across the table from
me several times throughout adulthood. I have shocked them
with my indifference to the stellar qualities they believed
they possessed—qualities they believed most women would
die for. They have been devout Christians whose homophobic rants over chicken Alfredo and breadsticks disqualified
them from friendship, much less a relationship. They have
been underemployed, brilliant intellectuals who I knew could

not afford their own share on the international trips I would continue to take with or without them. They have been emotionally damaged therapy avoiders who had stable careers and were ready to settle down with a wonderful woman like me.

Most women would have died for men like them. I chose to keep breathing.

There are women who work hard to get chosen. They sit across tables from men who bore them and then accept yet another date, because mediocrity isn't enough of a reason to rule out a man who appears ready to choose. They deny themselves sex in hopes that their chastity will yield a partner who will see them as superior to the women who remain unchosen, yet sexually fulfilled. They date just-divorced men, overlooking all the glaring reasons why these men's wives left them. They wait for these men to heal, praying that once the healing is done, they will be chosen.

There are women who are eager to compromise. They don't want to move to the other side of the country, but the man who has chosen them already lives there. They don't want to relinquish their Saturdays to swim meets and play dates, but the lord of the ring yearns for fatherhood. So, these women compromise.

For clarity's sake ...

Brenda and I believe in negotiation in all our relationships; we compromise for those who have our best interest in mind.

We are not impressed when men are nice to us because we expect basic human decency. We dole out this decency to others and tend to have it come back to us in most interactions. We do not find the black man with a job and a savings account to be a prize worth competing for because working every day and planning for the future are not extraordinary traits of adulthood.

It is not my intent to paint the women who are side-eyeing this entire section as less enlightened than me. I have no interest in examining and picking apart the institution of marriage, whether in its more traditional form or any modern version. I have no interest in analyzing how the institution traps (or doesn't trap) women into a life of fairy-tale myths that they will spend most of their partnership unlearning. Neither do I intend to waste my words debating the value of any of the plethora of patronizing blogs and "books" framed as advice to help me figure out why I am walking around in this world with a naked ring finger.

I am not married because I do not want to be. I am not married because I have not seen any iteration of the institution that inspires me to want it. To work for it.

A chance to get chosen does not move me.

I am single because I am enough for me.

4.

I HAVE ALREADY MADE MY CHOICE. DISCUSSIONS about its ramifications on anyone other than myself will not be entertained.

Brenda, Grace, and I have crawled down from the cross you have become so accustomed to seeing us nailed to, our bleeding hands and bulging eyes praised as holy sacrifice. Affix your gaze on that old, rugged cross; martyrs no longer hang here.

2

The S Word

*D*on't get me wrong, I respect Oprah. She is a good role model, but . . ."

The sixteen-year-old girl who was beginning her hesitant approval of the black woman who needs no last name had impressed me from the moment she walked into the Police Athletic League (PAL) in Hollis, Queens. I thought I wanted to be a comic. So I'd moved to the city everyone moves to when they think they want to be an artist. As it turned out, my pay-the-bills hustle was growing on me faster than my try-to-be-a-comic hustle. I was traveling around the five boroughs doing writing workshops in public school class-rooms and community centers. The work was giving me a perspective on New York City I don't think I would have gotten in any other gig. Which brings us back to the PAL facility in Hollis, Queens and the teenaged girl who was about to disparage Oprah.

Something about this young lady had piqued my interest when she walked in late and apologetic. She, like her peers, had some standard after-school job a few times a week and only did this program for "underprivileged youth" because it was a quick way to make a few more bucks without wasting a swipe on the subway. She wouldn't admit that she was drawn to the chance to improve academic skills she knew she had not fully honed even after many years of formal education; she postured as if it were just the $100 stipend she'd get at the end of the month that motivated her. The goal of saving up for the perfect prom dress—not the writing tasks that had to be rewritten the following week after reading my comments—was what brought her out each week, even in the bitterness of January.

But, unlike her peers, she was self-possessed. During discussions, there was an honesty hidden in her comments that disarmed me. She seemed unafraid to admit, in coded speech that her counterparts couldn't hear, that much of her posturing was bullshit and she needed more than the people in her life could give her.

"She has made all this money and is keeping it all for herself." The young woman shook her head as if she had just exposed Oprah as a suspected human trafficker. "I mean, you don't want to share your money with a husband? Okay, I can understand that, I guess. But not even kids? You don't want to even have your own children? So it's gonna be all about you your ENTIRE life?"

And then the S word was dropped.

It came from another student in the room and was accepted without hesitation by the self-possessed girl.

"It does seem selfish, huh?"

I was around these girls' age when that word was applied

to me with the same ease and for the same reason that she was now applying it to Oprah.

You are selfish.

When people my own age accused me of it, the implication was clear. To be selfish, specifically this type of selfish, was as shameful as if I had been called the other S word. The one the girls who wore too-short skirts and had too many exboyfriends in their brief dating history were called.

Adults, because they possessed more sophisticated shaming strategies, employed subtle tones to communicate that girls like me should not make it their goal to turn into women like me. "I remember thinking like that when I was young," they said, chuckling away my silly notion that I could grow into an adult human without bearing at least one child, regardless of how much I did not want one. "But, ya know, when you get older, your life becomes about more than just you."

You are selfish.

The word was quite effective in shaming me years ago. When I was still my students' age, it was expert at silencing me. I remember conversations that went along these lines:

Random Person: You know, when you have kids . . .

Me: I don't think I will be having kids.

Random Person: (blank stare, chuckle, or awkward silence) Well, you are still young, so I can understand why you'd be so selfish now, but you'll grow out of that.

This statement was often followed by a lecture of varying lengths that included: extolling the virtues of child rearing, pontificating on the trauma I must have experienced in such a short life to warrant my rejection of motherhood, and pointing out that I had never even known the joy of looking into my baby's eyes for the first time.

Me: Um . . . well, I don't know. Maybe it's just not . . . (silence)

I don't know why my younger self knew what the sixteen-year-old girls in my writing class also knew. If I could have found a rationale for choosing not to have children, I would have been allowed to speak. If I had said I was afraid of the sacrifice involved in parenting and not just unwilling to make it, I would have earned the right to continue to assert myself. If I had confessed doubt in my ability to be a good mother instead of my lack of desire to be one, this other person would have invited me into further dialogue. I needed some other motive besides my unapologetic selfishness. But the only reason I had for not wanting children was not wanting to put a child's never-ending needs before mine. And once I was assigned the descriptor of selfish, my only recourse was silence. I had been accused of the most horrid crime any non-male person could commit: to think myself so important that I would make decisions that guaranteed the person I valued most—me—would remain my top priority.

PAMELA IS A HIGH SCHOOL TEACHER IN HER THIRTIES. When she was younger and was accused of the horrendous crime of selfishness, the words she offered in response are proof that the point of using the S word was to shame the black woman who was avoiding motherhood. "I would get very irritated," she says. "And defend myself."

This defense took the form of résumé dropping. Pamela

ticked off all the ways in which she cared for her niece and nephew. She cited all the times she babysat when she could have been at home reading. She listed the expensive gifts she bought her preteen niece because she had disposable income. "I am the best auntie of any auntie that has ever auntied," she'd say, and in doing so reshape herself into the image her community needed to see. An image of a caretaker—one so nurturing she even cared for the children of others.

The more auntie accomplishments Pamela ticked off to a person who had accused her of selfishness, the more forgiving that person became of her rejection of motherhood. She didn't have her own children, but she was helping with other people's children. Yes, she was who they needed her to be. "The message that I had to compensate for not having my own children was clearly communicated to me, even when I was still in college," Pamela says.

At thirty-five, Pamela just chuckles now when the S word is flung her way. She finds the word and the person slinging it comically absurd. "Stop doing shit I can't do! Stop being this other type of black woman—one I never even thought about being!" But as a late adolescent, she knew from others' reactions that to choose herself for no other reason than wanting to live for herself was to reject some sacred agreement that the women before her had signed with Black America. A poorly drafted, binding contract with suspect explanations of benefits and no beginning or ending date that could be renegotiated.

"See, black folk love them some patriarchy," Pamela says without flinching. "Even though we been doing the shit wrong for generations, all the women cling to our twisted performance of patriarchal roles like it's Lauryn's final concert and she has pinky-promised to show up on time." Women get something for submitting and taking the shit of the community in a functional patriarchy. They pop out babies, care for them, and submit to husbands, and in return, those husbands protect and provide for them. The women take care of house and home and the men get to make grand, life-altering decisions that impact the lives of everyone in that home—"They lead their flock to the greenest pastures, like the pastor used to say when I used to go to church."

According to Pamela, black women often "submit" and "commit" to the requirements of female gender roles even when the men for whom they are having babies expect them to fulfill every other role in the house and community. "And then when you have the nerve to subvert the role of woman, to claim autonomy over your life, these women who are doing everything but getting little in return get big mad at you." Often, it is other women who throw out the S word with special, spit-laden disgust at we black girls who save up for our own tubal ligations and not our daughter's sweet sixteen party.

When I look back on the inappropriate questions and lectures I endured during my younger days, the most appalled and downright angry responses to my saying, "I don't want the lifestyle of a parent" came from women who had boasted about the pinky toe they'd given to their youngest (who needed a new one for school) and the right arm they'd ripped off from their shoulder (because their oldest had outgrown his during a baseball match). It is as if my voicing disinterest in their brand of sacrifice was somehow negating our entire culture's uplifting of this blessed sacrifice as moral superiority.

There have been many times when I've sought to avoid a random person's inquiry into my joyous, childfree life by choosing silence right after I answered "no" to "Do you have kids?" And yet, there have been more than a few times when the inquisition has proceeded along anyway.

SOMEWHERE IN MY LATE TWENTIES, RANDOM PEOPLE advising me about reproductive choices didn't change their line of questioning—I just changed my responses. I did not dare question the accepted narrative that motherhood was this beautiful gift from God from which all women would derive joy and pleasure. Although my observations of the child-rearing experiences of women of all races and backgrounds poked crater-sized holes in this narrative, I knew better than to suggest that, perhaps, children were not always blessings to women. There are few tropes about the sanctity of the black family that the person whose womb is used to create it are allowed to challenge.

In the absence of silence came my agreement with the person whose diagnosis of my life choice involved the S word. Many of the exchanges in my twenties and thirties went a little something like this:

Random Person: You don't have kids yet?

Me: Nope.

Random Person: Well, don't let it make you anxious. You still have time to meet a nice man and have some pretty babies.

Me: Naw, won't be doing that. I am all for meeting a nice man, but won't be having babies, pretty ones or ugly.

Random Person: (blank stare, chuckle, or awkward silence) Aw, come on, how can you say that? What woman wouldn't want to give her husband a child?

Me: So, a man who marries is entitled to at least one free human baked fresh in his wife's womb?

Random Person: Isn't marriage about compromise? And if you were in love, wouldn't you want to make this sacrifice for the man who loved you back?

Me: If I give him my commitment for life, he has gotten more than enough sacrifice from me. Perhaps he should marry one of those selfless women if he needs more than that.

Now in my forties, I am curious what other women like me hear when they are presented with the S word after yet another random person wants to know why they never had children or offers them encouraging words about breakthroughs in fertility treatments that could grant them the sacred gift of motherhood.

"What do I hear when someone calls me selfish?"

Dawn is in her forties. She is an educated, well-traveled black woman who didn't just forget to have children; on the contrary, she, like me, has had a decades-long allegiance to birth control that surpasses the love of good black men with whom she has been involved over the years. Her multiple methods of blocking sperm from sidling up next to even her homeliest eggs are far stronger than her mother's desire to be a grandmother.

"What I hear," Dawn continues, "is someone saying to a black woman, 'How dare you say no!' I hear anger that I value me over them."

Such audacity is appalling. A woman wearing black skin

saying no. To anything. A woman wearing black skin saying no to nurturing. Anyone. Well, those two acts of selfishness are worthy of pillory. But a woman wearing black skin saying no to nurturing and caring for children; *this* could justify the lighting of torches and assembling of mobs armed with pitchforks. A woman wearing black skin refusing to give birth to children? When she has no good reason for such a refusal? She does not have fibroids. No infertile husband. No worthless dude who wouldn't help her out in the first place. In fact, she has so many reasons to take on the role for which she is genetically predisposed: health care, a mature man itching for babies, family support (her mama been retired and would happily spend her days loving up on grandbabies!), and her job even offers generous maternity leave!

"Now, that's some next-level selfishness," Dawn says laughing.

These selfish women have the nerve to be content and skip around their daily lives. They turn down requests to babysit without offering long-winded stories of all the things they have to do that they can't get out of in order to watch their darling little nephews. They allow people to believe they are choosing to just lie on their couch and watch Netflix when they could be pushing their friend's toddler on a swing at the park. This is exactly what many of these selfish black women are doing: Reading books. Watching shows. Drinking wine. Spending hours lying in bed being spooned by the same men they are denying offspring. Sitting in cafés, drinking coffee, eating muffins and shit. Drafting business plans for their own start-ups. Writing words in journals. By themselves. ALONE, did you hear me?! Minutes, hours, days—entire cycles of not caring for children, of not even caring for the men who want to give them children.

"These heffas got the nerve to be happy." This conversation is taking place over the phone and I can see Dawn's face in my head. She has just rolled her eyes, registering faux-disgust. She clasps her imaginary pearls, signifying most of Black America's chagrined disapproval when black women exhibit joy in living a choice that is supposed to bring regret, a deep longing.

And we don't take the tribe's hints. We sit and watch these people toss out their versions of wisdom and let those pearls drop to the floor without blinking an eye. When we take our niece out for a mani-pedi and lunch, the women swarm around with reminders that "you would be such a good mother." And still . . . we keep right on not getting pregnant. When we show up at a toddler's Chuck E. Cheese party to eat reheated frozen pizza, we are served refried comments such as, "I am surprised you even bothered to come to this." We laugh along with the tribe, not concerned with the passive-aggressive accusations. And then, because we don't seem to despise the children running around, we are told, "You would not be a bad mother, ya know." Because we are happy to see a child make it through another year on this crazy earth, because we appear to enjoy hugging and treating this little human with warmth at the celebration of her birth, we are asked, "Are you sure you don't want one of your own?"

Yet we keep right on taking our pills and storing our condoms in cool, dry places. We keep smiling at weddings, dancing at parties, and even singing at church without a baby. Not one.

Next. Level. Selfish.

At forty, I barely notice the hundreds of ways in which other black folk call me selfish for basing my reproductive decisions on my needs only. I am absolutely fascinated with the implication of the word. When someone is called selfish, it suggests there should be some corrective behavior. There is also an implication that thinking only of self is a direct correlation to someone else being placed in a less-than-satisfactory position. For instance, my mother sometimes bought a family-size box of Popeye's chicken for my siblings and me as a special treat. Once, I didn't wait until everyone had eaten their fair share of the chicken before going back for my third drumstick. "Wow, that is selfish," my mother chided me. That descriptor, along with her disapproving look, was my mother's way of saying, "Because of your greed, one of my other children might go hungry."

She was right. I had three brothers and a sister with whom I was supposed to share this greasy treat. My behavior should have been corrected because it impacted several people's lives. My selfishness could have prevented someone else in our house from having his hunger satiated.

When women choose to be free of children, in contrast, what behavior is it that folk believe we should correct? We are told, "But your husband might want one! How selfish of you to make such a choice without thinking about your mate." It is implied that we have put our husbands—partners who do exist in real life and phantom men who "might" show up somewhere in the future—in a less-than-pleasing situation because we have chosen not to use our wombs to quench their baby thirst. We are asked how we can make such a decision when our parents only had one child: "Your mother won't have any grandbabies." It is implied that we need to rethink this notion that we are not causing pain to others when making autonomous decisions about our bodies.

Another ploy to correct the selfishness of childfree women is to insinuate that birthing and raising children venerates deities and memorializes ancestors. "Don't you want to honor Oshun?" "If you want to get your grandparents back, bring children into this world. They continue the fight our forefathers could not." Our selfishness also dishonors the supernatural and steals the legacy of the dead.

It is, in fact, my special place from whence this potential child will emerge. It is my life that will be the most changed, for better or worse. It is me who will have to make the harder sacrifices during the early years of this potential child's life. It is me who will be risking death simply by choosing to give birth. (FYI: Maternal mortality is not just a thing in "third world" countries. An unsettling number of women still drop dead in American hospitals while giving birth in the twenty-first century. And the number of black women, particularly, who take their last breath during delivery is appalling.)

Maybe I am stuck on stupid, but I need someone to explain to me in simple sentences why preservation of self should not be the key position from which the decision to bear a child is made.

THE GREAT GIFT OF AGING IS THE ABILITY TO RELEASE yourself from responsibility for others' reaction to you. The relinquishing of such burden comes with an additional prize: finding people's disapproval or shock about who you are ridiculous.

What has become truly entertaining for me are all the what-if questions I am asked. Although the inquirers use different words, they all are asking this question: When you say you don't ever want to be a mother, what do you mean by saying you don't ever want to be a mother?

What if your sister died in some freak accident and her husband also died (presumably in this same freak accident) and his mother also ended up dead and your mother and the people they had previously named as legal guardians of their children in case they both died in freak accidents all died too —then you would take your nephews in, right? You would become a mother under those circumstances, wouldn't you?

I mean, I know you keep claiming there is no circum-stance under which you would mother, but let's say you are walking past this dumpster and you hear a baby crying and you look into the dumpster and you see this innocent baby just thrown away like it's worthless? I know you would call the authorities and watch over that dumpster baby until they got there, but let's just say the authorities couldn't find any other person to take this baby. You know how there are thou-sands of infertile couples on waiting lists to adopt babies? Well, they all have died or just had miracle pregnancies . . . *Then* you would adopt that dumpster baby and raise it as your own, wouldn't you?

Okay, there are aliens from outer space who have kidnapped the cutest mocha baby with the biggest dimples you have ever seen. They are threatening to take this beautiful human baby back to their alien world and raise it as an alien unless *you* agree to adopt it as your own. Wouldn't you save that baby from the alien apocalypse? I mean, surely you would be less rigid about this childfree thing if it meant saving a baby's very humanity, wouldn't you?

THE "DOES YOUR HUSBAND KNOW" QUESTION RANKS high on Pamela's favorite of intrusive-questions-adults-should-know-not-to-ask list. Pamela married Lawrence three years ago. She had been dating for fifteen years by the time she sat down for a cocktail with Lawrence. Those many years of dating had made her focused and clear on who she was and who she needed to complement her life.

"I let Lawrence know on our first date I was not having children," she tells me. "I had had enough conversations with men who got in their feelings because I had no desire to bear the children they had just as little desire to raise to know I needed to state who I was up front."

Given this, when Pamela's rejection of motherhood somehow finds its way into conversations with people who assume all women long to be mothers, she is thrown off by these people's assumption that she signed a lifelong contractual agreement with a man without ever disclosing such a significant term of the deal to him beforehand. "They seem surprised that a man was able to see my loyalty to and love for him, my kindness, my fantastic boobs, my intelligence, my wit as enough reason to marry me. It seems astounding to some Lawrence was able to marry me just for me . . . just because he recognized I was awesome."

Married, childfree ladies get "Does your husband know?" Their single counterparts get this ridiculous version of the same question: "But what if it were a deal breaker for a potential husband?" This question has always seemed so rife with absurdity to me. So, a man wants you to carry a human life inside of you and then commit the next several decades to sacrificing for this human life? You couldn't just make yourself want to do it because he's nice and has a good job? I have answered this ridiculous question more than once, befuddled, by saying, "Well, if we were getting to the point where children were being seriously discussed, then marriage would have already been discussed. Wouldn't he know by this point that motherhood was not my thing? So, if he's asking, then he obviously has not been paying attention to the woman he has been dating all this time. Do men normally pop the question and right after think to ask, 'By the way, you believe in God or nah?'"

Dawn is convinced this is what equally confuses and enrages black folk about black women who are childfree by choice. So many black women have been convinced we have no other options for mates but black men. So many of us have been convinced that no matter how much we accomplish on our own merit, until we can prove we are not one of *those* black women, we have accomplished naught. *Those* black women are the ones who have become so wrapped up in being awesome on their own terms that they cannot figure out when and how to humble themselves before a true king.

"So what those people hear us saying is, 'I would even

choose myself over a worthy mate.'" It does not matter that this mate has not cited as his deal breaker something reasonable like living in Texas or date nights at Applebee's. To them, bringing a life you don't want into the world is a reasonable compromise to make for the ideal man. It is not beyond the realm of rational thought if you want to prove to your potential king and the royal court of Zamunda that you are not one of *those* black women.

This alternate universe beyond the realm of rational thought has been exposed to me several times in conversations with men who might have been potential partners. My most vivid memory of a baffled beau was a man whose every action—large and small—in daily life screamed of someone disinterested in the work of fathering. From the jobs he chose to take (and quit) to the noncommittal way in which he courted me at the very beginning of our relationship, it seemed obvious that being tied to a child for more than an afternoon would suffocate and kill him.

Yet when we hit the three-month mark and he asked the requisite, "You're not that into kids, are you?" he looked crestfallen when I stated that even if I fell in love with him and wanted to pursue something long term, I would still not want to have his children. "You should know," I said, trying to break it to him gently, "that you are the third man with whom I have had this conversation. Nothing has changed since the other two. I will not have any man's child. Ever."

A man who grumbled about rising from bed before 10:00 a.m. A man who had quit a job after only a month because "I thought it would be different than it was." A man who had made it to forty without ever becoming a father (not even one close call in his twenties!)—*this* man needed a moment to digest this news. I could love him, I could commit to being his woman, maybe his wife, and still have no desire to give him a child from the fruit of my loins? Whether he really wanted this hypothetical child I should, in theory, long to give him was irrelevant; somehow, my refusal to allow him voting rights on my womb made my proclamation of love mere lip service. Surely, I could not truly be in love with him, even if I said I was.

My beau asked for some time to figure out if he wanted to continue dating a woman who had no desire to give birth to a possible child he might possibly want to maybe someday parent. When he returned from his pilgrimage a few days later, he was clear he liked me too much to part ways, but admitted, "I never thought about it before, I guess. I just assumed I would have children, maybe? I never thought about if I wanted to, though."

And with those words, my beau granted me a brief glimpse into this magical male world where boys spend their formative years assuming they will be the sole star of their own adulthood mini-series. A world where you are never made to consider *if* you will be an eventual caregiver, just *when* you will be one. A woman's flat-out refusal to perform the role being the only catalyst for beginning to question if you want the job yourself.

It occurred to me that those times when he was visiting family who had brought young children along to the gathering, no adult had ever left him in the room with these children he had not given birth to and just assumed he would watch them until the parents returned. No one had advised him to choose a career based on how easy it would be for him to take care of children. When he was ten and pondering if he wanted to be a teacher or a movie maker when he grew up, I bet no one said to him, "I think you should choose teaching because you can be home by four, which means you will still have time for your kids." I was certain no grown-ups had ever automatically added "children and their care" to his list of adulthood responsibilities even before he had hit puberty and was able to create them. His arrival at middle age and only now having to consider whether or not to procreate provided the answer to my rhetorical question.

The beau and I had a couple of conversations throughout the years about my stance. A year or so in, we were watching television when he shared a story with me: He'd been in the drug store earlier that day and seen a couple with their young child. "He looked like he was about three," he recalled, smiling. The father was telling the son that if he could convince his mother to buy whatever junk food he was trying to swindle him into getting, he could get two of those treats. The boy was going over possible arguments with his father in hopes of winning this challenge. "It made me think," my beau said. "Do I want to totally give up on that? It was just such a nice thing to see."

I smiled as he relayed this story because it did seem like a pleasant moment to observe. "Yes, it is nice to see parents who are not exhausted or frustrated or overwhelmed. I saw something similar on the train the other day." I pointed out that I had not shared my story of semi-longing with him because there wasn't one to share. Two parents were playfully talking to their cute child. I looked at the child and smiled. I smiled at the parents and told them they had a cute child. I went back to reading my book. By the time the conductor had announced my stop, I had forgotten there was a cute child with loving parents also heading home on the train.

I wanted the man I now loved to know he had a dilemma he had to solve. "You have to figure this out, baby," I said. Then I explained to him that he had much more to lose than I did. Told him I'd been clear about who I was ever since the moment girls in my sixth-grade class, who had been discussing what they would name their future daughters, turned and waited for me to play this bizarre game with them. "If you wake up next year or next month having decided you want fatherhood," I said, "you will lose me." I wondered if I was being too harsh, yet continued anyway. "If you decide you love me too much to leave, you will lose the chance to be a father. You can't have both."

When we did split—amicably—we hadn't had a conversation about children and where he stood on having them in years. The relationship had, for many reasons, run its course. When a relative asked about the beau and if we were still together, I provided the modified explanation: irreconcilable differences. She gave me what I had come to expect as the you-must-be-one-of-*those*-black-women looks as I turned away and engaged with another person in the room.

Almost a decade prior, when this same relative had asked about the dissolution of a relationship, I'd explained how this man had wanted to be a father and I knew he would never get that as long as we were together. Eventually, he had accepted this, too, and moved on. This relative looked dumbfounded as she asked, "You mean, all that man wanted was a baby?"

The sheer shock that I could not just suck it up and give birth was overwhelming to her. How seriously was I planning to take this no-kids thing? What if another man came along and just wanted one measly offspring? Most men felt it was their right, once they had proven themselves father material, that the woman they loved give birth to their child. All these men wanted was babies? They weren't asking for elaborate meals, kinky sex? Just for me to birth and raise their children? And they were up for helping with the raising, too? And I was going to continue to deny them this?

At a spa in Kigali, Rwanda, I thought the latest random person to question my reproductive choice would punch me in the face. Years before moving to Africa, I had stopped making any effort to censor my disinterest in raising children and frame my joy with being childfree in ways that made other people comfortable. I had forgotten how much people expected me to capitulate to this universal narrative: women are meant to be mothers. So when, after answering the usual "Do you have children?" in the negative, the woman asked me why, I responded bluntly, "Because I don't want them."

I walked over to the other side of the room to pour myself another cup of tea.

"This is not true," she said. "You want children."

"No, I don't," I said, lifting my tea, "which is why I have made it to forty without ever once being pregnant."

A younger woman, who looked to be in her early twenties, tried to help me out by suggesting, "Not everyone is blessed with motherhood at the same time. My mother was still having children up until she was forty-seven."

I didn't take her help. I didn't need or want it.

"Your mother was having kids in her forties? Um . . . that makes no sense to me, but hey . . . to each her own." I pulled an ottoman from a nearby chair and plopped my legs on it.

The younger lady tried to help me understand the beauty of her mother's fertility well into her later years. I just smiled and offered, "We all make our choices, right? Hopefully, everyone is as happy with their decisions as I am with mine."

And then came the anger from the older lady who had been trying to show me with her heavy sighs and prolonged sucking of teeth how much she disapproved of my flippant dismissal of maternal instinct. She walked over to my chair and stood over me as I added another cube of sugar to my fresh cup of tea. She pointed her finger at me and waved it vigorously in the air, as if this would make me understand how important it was to voice allegiance to motherhood, and said, "I will claim it for you in Jesus's name."

I sipped my tea and stared at the lady, who looked like she was going into cardiac arrest. "Ma'am, Jesus has nothing to do with this. It is not his uterus."

When I tell parents or people who are childless by circumstance this story, there is a chuckle and a dismissal of the Rwandan woman's harmless meddling: "Well, you were in Africa, it's to be expected," they say with a shrug.

However, women who are childfree by choice, like Dawn and Pamela, react a bit differently. I can just hear either of them saying, "At least she kept her brand of bullying on Front Street." If there is one thing I appreciated about the reinforcement of traditional gender roles I encountered in many African countries, there was the lack of pretense that my choice should ever be accepted as a valid option for anyone who considered herself a woman. There was a refusal to even play along with the notion I had the right to make such a choice and still call myself sane. It was less emotional work to converse with this Rwandan woman who outright demanded that I be normal than it is to converse with Americans, who only hint at my abnormality and suggest my inferiority as a woman.

"I don't know why black folk here in America just don't tell us and even themselves why they get so mad when we don't even pretend like we buy this whole story about the blissfulness of motherhood," Pamela says. She insists there is a fear that if more black women stopped having babies and began using their resources on all the other avenues they often neglect in order to raise children, no one else would fund, feed, and fill up the community. There would be no motivation for black women who suffer nobly at the hands of everyone in their community to continue to do so if children did not chain them and their resources to that community.

"It's why childfree black women feel the need to go on about how much they love being around their nieces and nephews and how much they go the extra mile for their students when someone suggests they only think about themselves," Pam argues. "As long as we are fulfilling that expectation—to care for any and all children—then we keep funneling our energy, money, and time into a community that often does not replenish those resources. As a matter of fact, it just taps into the resources of another nurturing black woman when one woman's well runs dry."

That sixteen-year-old from my writing class in Queens is likely now one of those black women who is expected to step aside and smile when she sees someone heading toward her with an empty bucket. She should be a few years shy of thirty now. Who knows if she is a mother, a childless woman because of circumstance, or a woman who has consciously chosen to remain childfree? Who knows how many times—regardless of her maternal status—she has been whipped with the same word she lashed across Oprah's back and mine? I know the answer to that one: countless times, from the moment she refused to be the person someone needed her to be to make their life easier. The first time she said "no" to the person who loved the word "yes" just as much as they loved her. In that moment, the S word was draped around my student as evidence of her forgotten place, as a reminder that she needed to quickly step back into it.

"I am sure that girl was only parroting what her mama and aunties were saying around her for years," Dawn says. She is not bothered by this bright girl viewing an accomplished woman with agency over her life as being worthy of censure. For Dawn, there is no such thing as forming your own opinion when you live under your parents' roof. "For all their rebellious ways and assertions that they want to be their own person, teenagers really just mimic the values and perceived expectations of their families and the communities they grow up in." She tells me that girl was probably watching television while her aunties discussed the niece who was almost done with school and almost had an engagement ring on her finger but terminated her pregnancy because she wasn't ready for motherhood. "She heard Auntie Gert call that cousin selfish because she could have raised that child even though it would not have been easy. 'She killed that baby just because she didn't want to sacrifice even a little bit.' You know that is the tame version of what that child heard plenty times before she went to college."

Even I can hear Auntie Gert and her sisters critique this niece who chose herself over the collection of cells that could have become a human child. My sixteen-year-old student did not know she was hearing her aunties, either. She did not know that they were teaching her a valuable lesson—one she would one day either accept or question and reject.

"If she was as intelligent and self-possessed as you describe," Dawn reassures me, "then I am sure she at least questioned the narrative, even if she decided to end up living it anyway."

During that ten-week class, those faithful students and I did a little word study. We looked at root words and prefixes and suffixes to help them discover meaning of the difficult words that occurred in some of the texts we read.

I wonder if my student ever picked apart the word "selfish."

In Hollis, New Orleans, Compton, Charlotte, Harlem, Houston, black girls are sometimes chided for being too "womanish." Black boys get their gender-specific honorific for the same reason the girls do. When you are taking on the ways of an adult, you are acting woman*ish* or mann*ish*.

The suffix *ish* is key. It suggests the word "as" or "like." It is a simple man's simile. If you are womanish, you are behaving as if you are a woman. If you are mannish, you are acting like an adult male who has a set of expected behaviors and actions dictated by culture and community.

So, what about this *ish* when added to the root word self?

It is my hope that my student examined the word she initially intended as a criticism of Oprah.

She is self*ish*.

She is acting like herself.

Oh, what a precious privilege.

3

The Reality of Regret

My finger rested on the sentence in the novel and I kept waiting for a break in this group scolding to bring my fellow book club members' attention to it. "You see, it's different for men." I remain silent, as I know I am supposed to obediently listen to the familiar retort to the suggestion that women can, in fact, abandon their children with the same indifference as men: "Men don't actually carry the life inside of them. For mothers, our connection is natural; it occurs in ways that fathers cannot replicate."

I had learned to smile and nod well. Whenever someone corrected my cold-blooded suggestion that motherhood was not always viewed by every mother as a blessing, I listened politely as they used science-adjacent "facts" to disavow me of my cynical, childfree smugness.

When I was fourteen or fifteen and half-joked that if I ever ended up with a baby, a jail sentence for child abuse would follow, my mother almost dropped the can of soda she was sipping. "How can you even say something like that?!"

she demanded. "Stop joking about such things." Witnessing my mother's profound disappointment in my statement, I learned for the first time to make certain assumptions about women like the one my book club members and I were discussing. In the brief amount of time I had been old enough to notice, there had never been an absence of news reports of women who did what I had just joked about doing: abuse their children. Since I was a good person who my mother had raised with good values, these other women who had ended up as abusive mothers must be worse people than I was. Maybe they weren't monsters, but the evidence in their weaker morals lay in the harm they had inflicted on the vulnerable beings they were supposed to protect. These mothers could not be someone like me—a person who didn't need to give birth to know that the daily care of a child would feel more like a burden than a blessing, that it would be something that she could not do without some level of resentment.

"She just felt like she didn't deserve happiness, that's all." Another friend jumped into the discussion. She explained that the character in the novel had abandoned her daughter for some unknown reason other than what the sentence under my finger implied.

"Yes." I continued to smile as another book club member chimed in and explained why the sentence I was staring at didn't tell the whole story. "She deeply loved her husband, so when he died, she just felt like she didn't even deserve to be alive . . . much less alive with his child."

"But she didn't kill herself, though. She never even thought about it. She thought about leaving her child several times." I am patient as my fellow readers think about why this still is not enough evidence to support the idea that the character's motivation for abandoning her child was that she didn't want to be a mother.

These women are intellectual powerhouses. I stopped spending large amounts of time around those who aren't years ago. It doesn't take long for someone to offer, "Her brother-in-law was better at parenthood. The husband's brother seemed to get more joy from raising his niece, that's for sure."

"So you did read those parts, too?" I asked. I knew where this conversation would go because I'd had some version of it several times before. But it was still early into the afternoon. We still had two bottles of wine and an entire cake left to consume. Why not engage in a cyclical conversation that would conclude with everyone in the room trying to melt the ice from around my frigid, childfree heart?

"Like that time she left the kid at home alone. And when she came back she was happy to find her safe because it proved she could be left alone again. And when she thought this"—I lift my finger to make sure I have found the correct sentence—"She was ashamed to admit she was one of those women who did not find joy in motherhood at all." I look up at my friends and patiently wait for them to correct me (and the mother who had written the sentence I would be told I misinterpreted).

"But, yes . . . that is normal," one of the mommies in the room asserts. "A lot of women are scared and feel inadequate at first . . ."

"Do these women also talk about how much they dislike

having to put their lives on hold and just stop doing that altogether before they leave their child with someone else who wants to parent her?" I wait for further chastisement of my cynical interpretation of the actual events that happened in the book.

"She regretted that decision."

"But she never came back, though. Somewhere around Chapter 19 or 20, the author says part of the reason she was so consumed with guilt was because of how much she did not want to go back, how she was more ashamed of the lack of shame than of what she had done. Seriously, I am not even paraphrasing at this point. It's right there." I flip back to Chapter 20 and hold it up for the tipsy readers to see.

Rolled eyes and shifting of body weight are the only response to my counter-argument. The subject is switched to the portrayal of the woman's brother-in-law (and eventual husband) who ends up raising the child she left behind.

Regret is one of those worries that everyone has for the woman who consciously chooses not to have children. Sometimes, after years of not having a single soul check to see if we are over this phase of not wanting children, a friend will tell a random story of a woman she read about who waited too long to have children. "She thought she didn't want them, either." The friend will drop in this line as she stares at the childfree woman, searching her eyes for the pain that must be there. "Now she regrets waiting so long, because it is hard for her to conceive. Even with medical intervention."

There will be a pause as the friend again waits for the childfree woman to admit she is remorseful, that she has fantasized at least once about combing the hair of her little

Mini-Me and does feel a pang of jealousy when her friends share stories of watching their children open gifts on Christmas morning. The friend will read the childfree woman's silence as some sort of profound internal reflection, but the silence is really the woman's way of trying to figure out if her friend has been in a semi-comatose state for the last fifteen years when this same topic has come up and she has restated the same sentiment each time: "I won't change my mind because I know my mind well. How can I regret not having something I have never wanted?"

The friends and family who believe they have our best interest in mind worry about us despite the fact that examples abound of women who parent their children as if someone needs to counsel them on how to live happily (enough) with a life choice you regret. It has always struck me as odd that there is more focus on how remorseful women might feel about not having something than whether the women who do have that something feel like it was worth all the hoopla. Each time I have suggested there are women who regret having children, I have been met with such intense rejection, I wonder if what I really said was, "There are human mothers who eat their children's flesh for dinner and puree their skulls for the next day's lunch."

Aside from the prolonged "no, that is not what she meant" backtracking at the book club discussion, I was once shushed by a woman who was childless by circumstance. I have forgotten how we ended up discussing women who regret their decisions to be mothers, but I made a comment that was meant to show compassion for them: "For the average woman, standing up in this restaurant right now and admitting you screwed every man in this room and his brother in the same night would result in much less judgment than saying if you could do it all over again, you would not have your children."

The friend put her finger over her lips as she tried to shape my comment into the "right" one. "No, no, no . . ." She could barely get the opposition out. "I don't think they regret being mothers. They don't like how much it requires of them and sometimes how thankless it is. But, not *regret*."

I smiled and nodded through that conversation, too. It wasn't worth it to mention all the reading I had been doing that showed it was the experience of being a mother that some women regretted. Not the experience of being a single mother. Not the experience of being a mother with little help from your husband. Not the experience of being a mother to a child who had special needs that required more from you than you were prepared to give. Motherhood, period. They regretted choosing to raise offspring and were clear that if given the chance to reverse the clock, they would opt out. No matter how much the role was redefined and those obstacles that made it difficult were removed.

SOCIOLOGIST ORNA DONATH INTERVIEWED TWENTY-eight Israeli women who spoke candidly about their disillusionment with the motherhood experience. In *Regretting Motherhood: The Sociopolitical Analysis*, published by The University of Chicago Press, Donath frames the remorse with precision. She makes clear that all of the mothers appreciate their children's existence. The women in her study separated the people who their children were from the dissatisfaction they felt at the experience of mothering them. They loved their children and carried out their duties with the same dedication as women who relished in the role.

One of the participants, who went by the alias of Doreen, knew she would never speak about her remorse, especially to her children. She knew this feeling was something of which she should be ashamed, and yet: "I'd forgo them, totally. Really. Without batting an eyelid. And it's difficult for me to say that, because I love them. Very much. But I'd do without. There was a long period of time when I was seeing a psychologist. And it's funny. If there's something I feel utterly at one with, it's that."

Doreen stated what women are not supposed to feel, let alone voice to anyone (even under an assumed name). "Motherhood is not at all worth it. It is not something that brings me joy. I would not do it again knowing what I now know about how dissatisfying it is."

Each time Donath gave her participants a chance to explain their remorse in a way that implied a few low moments in an otherwise rewarding experience, the women were clear they knew what she meant by regret. It was the deep sense of loss one felt and sorrow that the thing lost could never be regained. They had felt this early into their roles as mothers, but they had kept these feelings of sorrow to themselves as they did the responsible thing: raised the children they had created.

These women ranged in age, socioeconomic background, and relationship status. Their children were young, older teens, and grown adults. Some had known they did not have the maternal instinct when they allowed themselves to become pregnant because it was a not-so-subtle requirement of their husbands and the culture at large. Some had never thought about not being a mother and just assumed when they became one they would enjoy it, or at least make peace with their responsibility.

What stood out for me as I read this paper was how much their experience resembled exactly what I knew motherhood would feel like had I allowed myself to be convinced to raise a child. All the women articulated their reasons for disillusionment differently, and how each came to identify what they were feeling as remorse was not always clear-cut, but Donath did note one common pattern: the women grieved the loss of themselves. The loss of freedom.

Many people insist that once you have children, you fall so in love with them that the things you have to sacrifice for them—your very self, for instance—fade into the background as you live in the fulfilling joy of shaping those children into productive adults. And here were these women confirming what I intrinsically knew: for some, the love of their children did not cancel out the remorse they felt because their life would never again be their own. They had fulfilled their duties to these children the way any decent human being would, but they were not those parents who believed it was all worth it in the end.

When I share these women's stories with my friend Natasha, she responds with compassion. "I won't judge them for this regret," she says, "because all women are different." I am surprised by her tone because Natasha has always been one of those friends who checks with me every five years or so just to see if I have come to my senses and become less adamant about rejecting motherhood. If there were anyone who I would expect to respond with as much pushback as my book club members had to my insistence that a fictional woman regretted her made up motherhood, it's Natasha.

She shares with me that many mothers do feel some remorse. The reason why she refuses to judge or question the Israeli women's regret is because she herself felt ashamed when three months after her first child's birth, she still had not bonded with her. "I knew there had to be something wrong with me," Natasha admits. When she describes those months of feeding her baby, comforting her as she cried, and snuggling next to her at night, she says she felt such a deep sense of shame because she felt no real attachment.

Natasha couldn't keep her fear to herself. The terror that she had committed the greatest immorality and had brought a child into this world that she didn't want. In a shaky voice, she asked her mother what could be wrong with her. Why did her husband seem to get so much more joy from holding their daughter than she did? Why was she relieved when someone else took the baby away from her and tended to her needs? Why, when she fed this cute little person she had carried inside of her for months, did it feel no different than when she waited tables in college and brought strangers their grand slams?

It turns out Natasha is paying her non-judgmental compassion forward. Years ago, her mother listened to her agonized confession and laughed. She assured Natasha there was nothing to worry about because "I felt the exact same way about you." She said that some women fall in love with motherhood right away, while others back into it. "There is no way to know which mother you will be until you have a child," she told Natasha.

But what if you are in that third category: a mother who never backs into motherhood? What if the three months turn into three years and then three decades? You have made it through the colicky nights. You have suffered through the early years when your child needs every part of you at every moment. You have survived the teen years, when even the most fulfilled mothers get driven close to the edge. What if your children have reached adulthood themselves, giving you time to reflect on motherhood, and you still feel the same way Natasha did as she waited for her husband to take this odd specimen off her breast and rock her to sleep?

If the answer is to be found in Donath's study, you assume what Natasha did, only worse. You must be a horrible woman—or, more mercifully, insane. Who does not find this, the greatest role a woman could play, fulfilling? One of the participants in Donath's study said she had a second child, in part, because she knew the reason why she didn't find it fulfilling the first time could not have had anything to do with the fact that she just didn't find much joy in parenting. She refused to believe that she was not fulfilled by parenthood. It took the second child for her to acknowledge that even though she had some happy moments while caring for her child, she was one of those women she'd had no idea existed: a woman who did not want motherhood.

"I get it," many who are childfree by choice say. We have been made to feel as if we were insane most of our fertile lives. We have been dismissed when we have suggested to prodding relatives and nosy strangers that we should be applauded for sticking to our guns because "women who don't want babies should not have babies just to see if they really don't want babies." When we refused to feign interest in the newborns our colleagues brought into the office for everyone to adore, the silent stares, followed by, "You really don't want to hold the baby?" reminded us that we were broken women. But these mothers who feel the exact opposite of what we have been assured we would feel if we stopped overthinking motherhood and just had a baby—they are confirming what we already know: having a baby would be a mistake we would not be able to rectify.

"I am not questioning your choice; I applaud it," a mother once told me. "All I am saying is if you eventually did have a child, because you are who you are, I am certain you would be a good mother. Good people become good mothers." This woman was childless by circumstance and had ended her journey of potential procreation at pregnancy. She had been a mother for more than five years when we were having this conversation. Like Natasha, she always spoke honestly about her lifestyle choice, often sharing how much she missed her childless life and disliked much of the grunt work that motherhood required. She was not one to concern herself with how other women lived their lives, so her comment on the mother I could have been was a passing observation, part of a larger conversation we were having about our peers now having more ways to define womanhood and to tailor their lives around that definition than previous generations.

I thanked this friend for saying I would be a good mother, because I knew it was meant as a compliment. "You, a compassionate and responsible adult, probably wouldn't turn into an evil, irresponsible one if you had a child. Chances are you would continue the pattern of kindness and wise decision-making you have followed all the years I have known you." It was an observation born from logic.

I would be a good enough mother if I allowed myself to be talked into becoming one. But would I be a mother who felt fulfilled by motherhood? Would I be a mother who was grateful I had become one?

Isabella Dutton seemed to be a compassionate and responsible person. In 2013, she wrote an op-ed for *The Daily Mail* in which she explained regretting entering into motherhood. She even went so far as to admit she resented her children.

Dutton was not having a dark parenting day when she wrote this piece. Each word is matter-of-fact. Each sentence calm. If it were a podcast, this confession would lull you into a nice afternoon nap. At fifty-seven, she was reflecting on how the truth she'd always known at her core was only proven when she'd done what good wives are supposed to do: given her husband the two children he wanted.

"I was acutely aware that a child would usurp my independence and drain my finances. I felt no excitement as my due date approached," Dutton writes. She went on to explain that the last few months leading up to the birth of her first child were not spent painting the nursery or stocking up on adorable baby clothes and toys; instead, she spent as much time as she could enjoying the freedom that motherhood would soon take from her. A cherished release from the constant responsibility of care she would never be able to claim again.

Dutton did not make her children suffer for her lack of fulfillment. She chose to be a stay-at-home mom so her son and daughter would have a full-time parent to care for them. She did not neglect or abuse them. She says, like every mother I have ever met, that she would have protected them from harm without a second thought and even wishes she could take on the multiple sclerosis from which her adult daughter now suffers. If she could spare her child pain, she would do whatever was required.

However, she also described those children as "parasites" who took so much every day and never gave back. She was not a woman with a high-powered career who gave up a chance to advance up the corporate ladder in order to be a mother, but still felt she would have been more fulfilled had she followed her gut and not had children. Going to work every day as a typist, coming home to eat a meal with her husband, and lying in bed with a good book as they fell off to sleep were the activities that would have brought her more joy over the course of her life than what everyone presumes women need if they don't want to wake up one day feeling empty: children.

"This duality doesn't surprise me," Kimya Dennis says when we talk about this seemingly contradictory claim. "I love my children, but I wish I had not had them."

Kimya, an assistant professor at Salem College, has begun teaching a course on women of the African Diaspora who choose to remain childfree. A criminologist and sociologist by training, she wanted to make visible the population of women who were like her, and she saw an opportunity to make such women the focus of more academic discourse.

"Whenever I have Planned Parenthood come in to talk for one of the lectures, the students get so comfortable with them there." Kimya has the organization's staff visit not only to highlight the nuances in women's reproductive choices but also to allow the demographic of her class (mostly working- and lower-middle-class women of color) an opportunity to safely articulate a version of what Isabella Dutton expressed in her *Daily Mail* piece.

"One semester when I taught the course there were two mothers in it. They talked about the importance of the abortion services Planned Parenthood offers." Kimya says it was the mothers in the Childfree by Choice course who listened the most intently during that one lecture when the staff at Planned Parenthood led the discussion. These mothers shared with the non-mothers in the room that they had not thought long and hard enough about what they would have to give up to raise children. "I heard them say that if they knew then what they know now," Kimya says, "they weren't sure if they would have carried their babies to term."

And yet there is no concern for these women. No worried loved ones who check in every few years to make sure they don't wish they could get a do-over. Perhaps these women need advice more than we, the childfree, do. Perhaps, if a space existed for them to seek it, they would invite suggestions on how to channel this remorse they can do nothing about. There is just as much chance that these mothers in Kimya's course could grow into Isabella Dutton as there is that they will consider motherhood the best choice they ever made.

When Kimya tells me about the mothers in her class

talking about whether or not they would remain childfree if they could do it all over again, she repeats two words: "safe" and "judged." She says the reason the women opened up in her class was because they felt safe. She didn't get the impression that the conversations about remorse could have happened in any setting with any group of people. Because of the atmosphere created by her guest speakers, the class felt like they would not be judged for voicing their honest doubts that carrying a baby to term made a woman happier in the long run than terminating the pregnancy. "They knew they would not be judged for what they felt," Kimya says.

When I first began researching this group of women, I noticed the similarity between their experiences and mine. If you scroll through threads on one of the groups on social media created for parents who regret becoming parents, someone will repeat some version of this statement: "There is no one else I can say this to because they will think I am a heartless person or try to convince me I don't mean what I mean." Many of the posters in these groups not only use cutesy internet handles with no resemblance to real names, they also choose avatars to use as their profile pictures instead of real photos of themselves. Publications from *The Guardian* to *Marie Claire* to *Vanity Fair* to *Jezebel* to *The Independent* have run articles within the last few years in which women, under assumed names, told journalists, "I feel awful for saying this, but I know it was a mistake. And I won't ever say it to anyone else because I know what they would think of me. The same thing I would think of them if they said to me, 'Having kids was my biggest mistake.'"

It makes perfect sense to me that a woman would wish

she had never given up her life even though she now has a beautiful life that bears her smile. It would strike me as odd if every single woman believed that the rewards of being a mother outweighed the near-death experience of childbirth, the constant sacrifice of self with little gratitude from the ones you are giving up so much for, and the lack of guarantee that they or the men you conceived these children with would ever return this level of sacrifice. I often find myself in this conversation with other women who are childfree by choice. Why is it so hard for people to believe that we never felt the desire to procreate? I never felt the desire to go to medical school and no one seems floored by that; no one is checking in with me today, years after I said I wanted to work in media, to see if I still have that application to Johns Hopkins, "just in case."

If Natasha is not surprised by women being remorseful about having chosen parenthood, then why were the members of my book club reacting to my interpretation of the novel we had read as if I had spoken ill of their very own mothers? If numerous publications are finding women who claim regret about what they thought they would view as their greatest accomplishment, then why were the comments sections of these publications dripping with rage and shock, complete with these women being called everything from selfish children themselves who did not deserve motherhood to cold-hearted bitches who needed to keep their truth to themselves?

We, in the media-saturated age of nothing being proven as fact until an attractive celebrity tells us so, must need to see the Isabella Duttons and Donath-style case studies more often on the big and small screen. Every now and again, Jennifer Aniston writes an open letter to the tabloids that says, "Listen, I am not pregnant nor do I want to be. Stop reducing women's lives to whether or not they have children. It's dumb and very 1956." For a few weeks after this, think pieces emerge that celebrate women who have chosen to remain childfree. Social media applauds Jennifer's much-needed reminder. We start to think, *Maybe there's more to this non-motherhood story than sad women who try to, but can't, have babies.* Do remorseful mothers need their own Jennifer Aniston? If one brave, beautiful starlet said, "I love my child *and* I know I should not have become a mother," would fewer people melt into puddles of wet rage when regular women said the same thing?

I WAS ON AN INTERNATIONAL FLIGHT THAT OFFERED the masterful film *The Hours* as a viewing option. I had seen this film in theaters when it first came out over ten years ago and remembered it had Meryl Streep and Julianne Moore in starring roles. I recalled Nicole Kidman was either Virginia Wolfe or Sylvia Plath in the film. The plot and storylines were fuzzy to me now, but I was certain it was a worthwhile re-watch. I pressed play, eager to remember what I had enjoyed years ago. For the first twenty minutes of the film, Julianne Moore's character, a stay-at-home mother in the 1950s, sleepwalks through her house as if she is heavily medicated or on the dangerous end of the autism spectrum. She goes to doctors and gets all kinds of treatments to help her with this mental disorder we are to infer is causing her difficulty with being a good mother to her son. By the middle of the film, I remember that Moore will abandon her husband and children. Meryl Streep's ex-husband in the movie is Moore's adult son, who writes scathingly about his mother's abandonment in his novel.

I am surprised that this is not the first thing I remembered about the film when I chose to watch it again. There have been so few times when I have seen any woman in a movie reflect my own extreme disinterest in caring for children, so you would think this portrayal of a mother who abandoned her children without regret would remain vivid in my mind. As I watched the movie again, I realized why I had forgotten about Julianne leaving her children and then telling Meryl she felt bad only because she didn't want to come back to them. The entire beginning of the movie, Julianne was portrayed as insane. She stared off into space when she was supposed to be making a birthday cake. She woke up in the middle of the night and stood out in her yard watching the sprinkler moisten the grass. She would be in a trance-like state when her young son came outside to ask her what was wrong. Whatever her mental disorder, it also caused her to forget what she was saying in mid-sentence, throw a newly baked cake in the garbage, and drive off to the store to buy a pair of gloves.

We, the audience, could decide it was not motherhood itself that she struggled with. The woman suffered from some illness that was only heightened because of the isolation of 1950s motherhood and the expectation to perform her role with no complaint. Maybe, if she were a modern-day mother who had outside interests (or even a job) and a husband who was an equal participant in the daily care, she would not have been so dissatisfied. Perhaps she would have wailed her remorse to Meryl had the circumstances of her motherhood experience been different.

Could we have handled Camille Billops's rejection of motherhood on the big screen? Billops, an artist who has curated her own work and the work of other black artists, as well as produced political and artistic documentaries for over three decades, abandoned her four-year-old daughter in the 1960s. She was in her twenties and the relationship with the child's father had dissolved, as relationships sometimes do. Camille was not floating around through life in a dead-eyed trance, looking confused when her child asked her to do simple things. Although her child's father had abandoned her and his baby, when Camille placed her daughter up for adoption, she was not the stereotypical single mother on welfare who had to stretch government cheese through two weeks of meals. She had graduated college, was working on her art, and had a respectable nine-to-five job that allowed her to live, if not lavishly, certainly comfortably. She had friends and family as a support system, too.

"I just didn't see what was so special about being an unwed mother," Camille admitted. She did not berate or abuse or even display resentment toward her child. She kept a responsible, trustworthy baby sitter on hire and went about her life as if she had no baby. But around her fourth year as a mother, she realized she was not developing any more joy for the role than she had the first year, and she decided that if she did not want to be her daughter's mother, it would be better if she found someone who did. Camille did not throw away a birthday cake she had just baked and meander around her living room as if she were coming down from a weekend weed binge. In her full and focused mind, she went to an adoption agency and found her child a family who wanted children.

Camille would probably laugh at these words I have written. My verbose pondering about why people are so surprised that women could do what she did and even in their old age still say, "I never regretted it."

Eventually, the daughter she gave up for adoption came looking for her. Camille, the consummate artist, and the man she had married in the years since the adoption made a documentary about her and her estranged daughter's attempt to establish some sort of relationship. The documentary, *Finding Christa*, won the Grand Prize at Sundance Film Festival in 1991.

The success of the documentary led to several opportunities for Camille to talk more about the decision she had made to put her daughter up for adoption. "You can't just not want to be a mother, like men just decide they don't want to be fathers," Camille said in an interview with the *Los Angeles Times*. Everybody wanted a reason. From family to virtual strangers, they wanted to know what she could have possibly been going through to get to the point where she would voluntarily hand her child over to someone else to raise. She was expected to supply sadness, at the least, in the absence of acceptable reasons. "If you just say you are sorry, we can forgive you," people insisted. If only she could be more tortured by her choice. If only she could have been the one to go in search of her estranged daughter instead of the other way around. If only she could admit to at least one sleepless night. One afternoon in the park in which she watched children at play and felt a pang from her ovaries that made her pray she would be given a second chance at motherhood. If only she had gotten pregnant again. If only she had shown that it was this particular motherhood experience—being left alone to raise a child when she was young, with a head full of artsy dreams—that she had rejected and not the motherhood experience altogether.

In the interviews Camille did during the promotion of *Finding Christa*, she spoke of the "truckloads of shame" people projected onto her for doing what she saw as a selfless and responsible thing: not subjecting an innocent child to a mother who did not want to be a mother. Not *her* mother. But *a* mother.

No one needs to have it explained to them why the women in the Regretting Parenthood groups don't use their names or pictures. The only thing surprising in the comments following the latest confessional from a mother who regrets her decision are those by more compassionate readers who, rather than disparaging the remorseful mother, chastise the judgmental and wish her peace.

When I was still in my early twenties, I feared I would one day realize I was wrong in all this silly "no baby" talk. For years, I waited to be kept awake by the ticking of my biological clock. I allowed people to speak to me as if I were a child, claiming to be concerned that I was misunderstanding my own desires and disregarding the advice of those who understood them better.

The mothers who are no longer remaining silent about

the regret I was supposed to feel seem to be sentenced to the same punishment. Their humanity and sanity are questioned, their honesty called selfish, depraved, and another sign of the crumbling of civilization. They are subjected to the public stoning women must endure when we are unsuccessful at forcing ourselves to live the myth the world has written as truth.

4

My Vote Is Valid

I remember the first time I chanted *nam myoho renge kyo*. It was like a return to a home I'd never known I owned. My introduction to the Soka Gakkai International and its practice of Nichiren Daishonin's Buddhism felt so right that a week later, I threw myself into further study of the Daishonin's teachings. I craved even more fellowship with this community of practitioners who committed themselves to their own human revolution and the realization of world peace.

I also remember the first time I chanted *nam myoho renge kyo* in my mother's house. It was different than the freedom I had felt when I had done it in my own apartment several states away. Home for the Christmas holidays, I whispered the life-affirming title of the Buddha's highest teaching and wondered if my mother could hear me. Hoped that she would not walk pass my room right as I was reciting the chapters from the Lotus Sutra, which was often the halfway point in my morning prayer routine.

Admitting that you do not believe in Jesus's ability to save you can be tantamount to saying your grandparents' stories of difficult times that God got them through could not have happened. Questioning the notion that a supernatural being called God is the source of your power is akin to questioning your parent's authority when they punish you. To denounce your duty to worship this god and give him ownership of your life is the equivalent of cursing out your parents. It is just not done. Even by those adults who, although they do sit in church pews a couple times a year and sing along to their favorite hymns, don't really believe in this afterlife and whose allegiance to God is about as solid as their commitment to any brand of any item they can purchase.

I was a teenager when I began to entertain the idea that this judgmental god who had dominion over my life did not exist. I found reasons not to go to church soon thereafter. Still, I gave lip service to my belief in this superpower in the sky who held my fate in his hand. Even today I will jokingly exclaim, "Fix it, Jesus," when I feel frustration over one of life's many mini-traumas.

Jamila Bey, a journalist who writes and speaks about atheism and humanism, assures me I was not the only one pretending. "The churches are filled with us," Jamila assures me. As part of the African Americans for Humanism network and host of the podcast *Sex, Politics, and Religion Hour* (*SPAR*), she has been vocal in her disbelief that the Judeo-Christian's god is anything other than a raging murderer at worst, a petulant toddler at best. Since coming out as a nonbeliever, she has encountered many African Americans who secretly admit, "Girl, me too" when she says she does not be-

NO THANKS | 63

lieve in this supernatural being who has more dominion over her life than she does. Jamila maintains that we are supposed to say, "Oh yes, this being is real," but, many of us believe otherwise. Even though we like to pretend we are not saying two different things, we prefer never to think about how the lip service we give to the belief to which the majority of our tribe subscribes does not mirror our thoughts and actions.

I WAS WITHOUT RELIGION UNTIL I WAS THIRTY-FOUR years old and discovered one that made sense—one that told me it was not only okay but required that my loyalties lie with fellow human beings and not supernatural ones. One that gave me permission to speak out loud what my former religion made me feel I could only whisper to myself: I am in charge of me. None other than me is the master of my destiny.

I was well into adulthood when I embraced a spiritual practice different from the one I was born into. I had been living on my own, paying my own bills and making my own decisions for at least one full decade before I said, "No thanks" to my parents' brand of religion and sought out my own. I was not just grown. I was *grown* grown.

So, why was I cowering in a corner of a room in my mother's house practicing this spirituality as if I were a half-naked tenth grader whose boyfriend was hiding in the closet?

For me, as for many, to reject my family's religion is to reject my family itself. That is why many nonbelievers will at the very least go to the big events with their families: christenings, Easter programs, Christmas cantatas. For Black Americans, it can be social suicide to reject the ritual of church—even if you don't participate in this ritual. To reject not only Christianity but its construct of god, too, can be asking for excommunication from your family and friends.

There is a social safety net in the tradition of church. It has given people like me a shared understanding of holy idioms (please refer back to my reliance on calling on Jesus to fix any number of trite wrongs I witness daily). In any circle of black friends who come from differing socioeconomic backgrounds and regions of the country, weekly church service and the routines surrounding it are often the common ground on which those friends will identify. Those friends would be able to sing the proper rendition of "Precious Lord," pausing at the same time, changing inflection and tone in the middle of the same verse. This would happen with little direction or rehearsal.

The black church is also, quite often, where many people, regardless of spiritual belief, can find concrete help in times of trouble. Although I have not been a participant in church culture in at least twenty years, I still participate in black culture. My connection to peers who are still involved (in large and small ways) in church has shown me how many churches have thriving ministries that service the poor and disenfranchised. Even those of us who don't believe in the doctrines of Christianity are not so shortsighted as to underestimate the real purpose a true church of Christ can serve in any community's life.

But to believe in the goodness of people who practice a faith is not the same as believing in the basic tenets of that faith. Who would question the validity of the homeless ministry? Express doubt about the importance of progressive church programs that help ex-convicts find work to reduce recidivism? There are many parishioners, however, who doubt the existence of a literal heaven. There are a number of semi-regular attendants of church service who only come for the comfort of the choir, never examining how this god being is not something they consider a tangible thing in whose hands their fate should be placed.

Since airing her *SPAR* podcast, on which she has featured other nonbelievers, as well as using her platform in media and journalism to write about secular humanism, Jamila has often had it confirmed that the closet humanists remain silent for (what they believe is) a good cause. "I'm not gon' say nothing, cuz I can't kill my grandmama. I might not hear from her ever again if I tell her I'm going to stop going to church altogether." The people who have said those exact words to Jamila laugh, but we both know there is little hyperbole in their fear that to live with integrity could result in either Big Mama's death or—worse—her rejection.

Jamila is certain that fear of being cast away by family is the biggest reason why people in the nonbeliever community continue to pretend as if they believe even when every single action, every single skipped church service, provides overwhelming evidence that they don't. We believe it is our queer brothers and sisters who get cast out; in truth, they are easier targets, and in the more fundamentalist Christian households they are excommunicated from the family as a unit—even if they still maintain meaningful interactions with individuals within that unit. While we nonbelievers do not risk the same level of rejection as LBGTQ family members, the reasons we remain in the closet are similar. If we are found to be too dif-

ferent, too far off from the accepted norm, we will be pun-
ished for it. Sometimes, just being labeled crazy is more than
enough to convince us, we who need the camaraderie of our
community, that voting outside its spiritual platform means
we cannot be accepted as a legitimate part of the unit.

And I say this as a New Yorker, who is often around people from different ethnic backgrounds as well as spiritual beliefs. None of my black friends go to church regularly. Many
don't go at all. But if you asked them all about god, they
would pledge allegiance, in some way, to his existence and his
omnipotence.

As I have become more cognizant of my own spiritual
beliefs, I have found myself in casual conversations with
friends about the idea of god. What I often find in these
conversations is the sentiment that Jamila notes as a diplo-
matic way to not reject what you were taught, but also not
express sincere belief in this god's power over your day-to-
day living.

Kimberly Veal, another popular voice in the Black Nonbelievers Movement, sums it up with this statement: "Nobody wants to say Mama led them astray." Because even
those non-tithing backsliders who claim to be "spiritual, but
not religious" are aligning themselves to the family value:
there is a being that is higher, greater than me. It is an emotional compromise similar to the one a good daughter makes
when she decides to never examine how her mother's shaming of her for being a young adult who wanted to explore her
sexuality damaged her long-term sexual development well
into adulthood. Mama employed the shaming strategy for
her daughter's best interest. *She didn't want me getting preg-*

nant for some no-'count boy, so she shamed me for being sexually curious and encouraged me to be afraid of acting on that curiosity. For these same black children, there is no need to think too deeply about whether they believe in this supernatural being who will one day hold up their lives for his judgment. Or if the cultural encoding of the Christian god structure is as beneficial for them individually and the culture collectively as we all have been taught it is. *Mama told me to "keep my legs closed and stop dressing like a ho" and look, I am a successful woman with a good career, good husband, and good (enough) kids as a result. Mama told me to trust in God because he is my power so look, I now trust in God and am very powerful.*

And that is the blessing and curse of a community's fight for survival under a brutal white supremacist system. It makes individuals loyal beyond logic to a belief structure that is supported by not only your own mother but also many in your family of all other black folk. I watched this deep cognitive dissonance repeatedly play out as scholar Dr. Stacey Patton regaled her Facebook followers with tales of researching and writing her book, *Spare the Kids: Why Whupping Children Won't Save Black America.* She shared summaries of the decades' worth of research showing the connection between early sexual behaviors and children whose bodies had been compromised by hitting when young. She provided anecdotes from sociologists and scientists who presented evidence-based theories about varying levels of brain damage resulting in compromised critical thinking in adulthood as being directly linked to those adults having been hit when they were children whose brains were not fully developed.

Dr. Patton spent over a year doing meticulous research

on the impact of spanking on children, providing study after study refuting the argument that "we gotta beat our kids so the police won't." She made this argument: Here we are in the twenty-first century still trying to get police not to murder our children like dogs in the street. After beating these same children for generations, white supremacy still ain't let up one bit. Is this not enough to convince us that beating children won't make them respectable enough in the eyes of the police who shoot them at first sight?

Intelligent, educated black men and women responded on Dr. Patton's threads with comments that fell into one of these categories:

1. Science is for white people.
2. My mama whupped me and I am a doctor now.
3. There is a difference between whupping and abuse. I am down for whupping, but not for abuse.
4. Jesus said beat your children or they will grow up to be murderers.

I watched black adults loyal to their parents refuse to admit those same parents instilled damaging practices into their psyches. Even parents who stressed they had stopped the cycle of compromising children's body integrity with their own offspring argued for why "I wouldn't be who I am today if my daddy hadn't put that belt to good use." A similarly dogged commitment to the supernatural being who holds us in servitude to him is also espoused by critical thinkers whose actions seem to refute a real belief in this god's power.

When I suggest that allegiance to this invisible god is, for many, just a standard assertion and not a deeply held belief, Jamila confirms that her own prodding of devout Christians as well as passive spiritual-but-not-religious types has revealed that they don't have much belief in this god's power. "When you ask what would they do if they came home and their house was on fire, they would respond by confirming that it is other humans they would call on." They would first run into the house, if that were an option. They would yell to a neighbor to call the fire department as they were running, the neighbors would do as they were asked, and then human beings with the appropriate training would show up to save the day.

"These people might mention saying a quick prayer before running into the house or yelling for help, but it is the humans they will rely on to do the saving," Jamila says. She maintains that asking for God to intervene is as knee-jerk a reaction as asking for his blessing on the behalf of someone who has sneezed.

Many, if not all, believers would maintain that the god being is acting through the human ones, which means the prayer to him would have worked. I do not know any believer in any deity-based faith who thinks the god to whom they pray is a magic wand whose power requires no action. I recall a verse in the Christian holy book that advises Christ's followers to take action because "faith without works is dead."

If there is anything to be said for nonbelievers, it is that we simply don't believe there is a need to say a prayer to an invisible being who activates the action of the visible ones walking around us each day. We believe humans are at the beginning and end of every miracle. Yet we sat in church for years feeling like blasphemous imposters for enjoying other humans' fellowship but doubting every word they believed with all their hearts.

DR. ANNALISE FONZA WAS A UNITED METHODIST clergywoman serving as a pastor to congregations in Missouri, Illinois, and Massachusetts when she decided to admit she no longer believed in the church's teachings. It took several years of further awakening to realize she did not believe in a supernatural deity at all.

Annalise's study in seminary school influenced her nonbelief. "I always say those people who call themselves Christians should go to divinity school," she says. Her program required her to study ideologies on Christ and his teachings. It was through those theologies that, she says, "I educated myself out of any religious need." She had always been an intellectual with a penchant for curious skepticism, so she doubted that the Christian teachings were the most correct about Christ and his purpose. She did not believe that Christ died for her sins. It was in divinity school where she discovered her doubt about the concept of sin: "The whole idea of atonement felt false to me. I knew I didn't believe it." Annalise felt she had no choice but to resign her post as pastor; she was no longer qualified to lead believers in the Methodist church.

There was no agonizing. No shame. No fear. It was a decision born from logic. If you do not believe in the concept of sin—an acceptance that even though you have not harmed another person or committed a wrong against yourself, you should feel some sort of remorse for dishonoring this god being—then you cannot call yourself one who believes in Christianity. If you do not believe you must seek atonement by prostrating yourself in front of that god's throne and asking for his forgiveness, then you are not a Christian.

For Annalise, returning her divinity credential was common sense. If people who eat bacon and routinely grill up lamb chops cannot claim vegetarianism, people who do not believe in the foundational tenets of the Christian church cannot claim Christianity, much less lead a congregation of folks who fervently believe in salvation through Christ.

When I hear stories like Annalise's, I am reminded of why Christianity never felt right to me. Why when I became a young adult, I found myself still appreciating the community and the common ground many African Americans felt by our near universal experience of going to church, but knew I did not believe the actual stuff the pastor was saying.

This was in addition to the disturbing homophobic denouncements that sometimes found their way into sermons. Or the gentle reminders that my place as a good Christian woman was one of special servitude to all the human men around me in addition to the supernatural one who was going to save me (if I behaved myself). The premise of Christianity struck me as being as ridiculous as it was offensive.

There was this magical place in the sky. Death might be my ticket to it. If I were good—and the criteria of that was unclear—I would be rewarded with no pain, no suffering, none of the challenges of human life here on Earth. The rubric did not base its assessment on the simple goal of avoiding harming anyone and being certain to help everyone. Random things that seemed either benign or non-issues would get my (possible) ticket to the magical place of no pain revoked.

Wait . . . wha?

This man named Jesus left this supernatural place to live a life of perfection on Earth. He was human, yet perfect. Therefore, he was the ideal role model as I pursued the path that led to heaven. As a human. Doing human things. Which meant fallibility. Flaws. You know, the key indicator that one is, in fact, human.

Huh?

My first act of sin occurred when I took my first breath. I crossed the mark against my own back by being born. I started out my life in a cage of sin that I did not construct yet was still culpable for, merely because I was born. Groveling for forgiveness for some misdeed I was not aware of was required of me. I could only gain salvation through subjugation.

Da fuck?

In conversations with Annalise, Jamila, and Kimberly, I learned it was not only me who felt as if being a good Christian called for you to suspend your belief in reality and go along with the fantasy the way one did when watching *Star Wars*. While I never witnessed any elder in the church admonishing members for asking questions, I do recall the lack of logical answers to such questions being dismissed as irrelevant to one's ability (or duty) to serve this god and his church.

"I was told that logic had no place in the church," Kimberly said in a lengthy conversation about her road to embracing atheism and humanism. Like many self-possessed, chatty black women, we became easy friends within fifteen seconds of our first conversation. When she mentioned that an actual adult with an actual mind had told her the use of that mind was not necessary in spiritual practice, I blurted out, "You a damn lie, girl. Passa and 'nem ain't never came right out and said that to you!"

I was wrong. Not only did someone say those exact words, her work in the behind-the-scenes running of churches in several American cities had further underscored the sentiment. When Kimberly was involved in church, she took the edict to "study God's word" seriously—and when she did, she concluded that "stuff still wasn't adding up." She does not begrudge Christians their right and need to believe in this god being. She, like Annalise, simply educated her way out of her belief in him, concluding that such a belief was illogical.

Jamila experienced none of the trepidation many nonbelievers recall when they decided a life of integrity was preferable to a life of appeasing the tribe by pretending they believed all the words they sang in the church's hymnal. "So, there's a man in the sky who loves me and unless I anger him, he will continue to love me?" she says. "That's abusive." For Jamila, what others found hopeful and energizing she recognized as condescending and oppressive. There were no anxiety-ridden conflicts when she became an adult and spoke the thoughts she knew she was not allowed to discuss as a child. "The Judeo-Christian god basically says you are worthless, you have no value, you are here for my edification. The only thing that is redeemable about you is that you love me." For Jamila, rejecting this abusive jargon that folk sang blissfully about every Sunday was inevitable. "If you say you are enough for you, that this god being is not the source of your joy, your accomplishments, your moral code, then you know you are not a Christian."

Much like Annalise, the logical progression of Jamila's religious education was to no longer claim she subscribed to it. That progression would also lead to embracing labels such as "secular humanist" and "atheist" because, just as one plus one equals two, her thoughts and actions equaled a person who did not believe in the supernatural and whose moral code centered around a reliance on humanity.

I HAVE SUBSCRIBED TO THE HOUSTON ATHEISTS Channel on YouTube. I happened to find a video on the channel that features black panelists who live in the heart of the Bible belt talking about what it is like to live in their skin without a need for or belief in the construct of god. Although many stories are shared in the hour-long video, a common undercurrent in every experience is, "It didn't make sense and I knew I could not say it didn't make sense."

In this video, I hear people like Jamila, Kimberly, and Annalise speak forthrightly about not fighting the knowing voice that whispered, "Wait. Wha?" before it articulated, "This is foolishness." I am amazed there wasn't any fear about walking away from it. Yes, it makes sense to not claim a belief system you knew to be untrue. However, communities of color rely on everyone believing in the church—even if the humans who run it are doing enough human things to obstruct its mission. So many grandmothers need for us to say "God willing" after we state an intended goal and "all praises to God" when we achieve that goal. But what if you don't believe god's will is greater than your own determined effort? What if you, like Beneatha in *A Raisin in the Sun*, believe that it is man's responsibility and well within man's capability to accomplish man's mission?

Well, you get slapped back into place by matriarchs who need you to mind.

"I told my grandmother I didn't believe in god just last year," one of the black atheists in Houston shares. "She just smiled and said, 'Yes, you do, baby.'" This man goes on to assert that while he is not interested in winning anyone over to his side, he does not, in fact, believe god exists and this is why he no longer goes to church. But his grandmother continues to pat him on the head and remind him that yes, he does believe in god and will someday return to church. "The lake of fire was referenced with that same smile on her face," he says.

I chuckled as I watched this man tell his story because twenty years ago, when I was discussing with a college friend my growing disbelief in god and the salvation promised by his son, he admitted the same doubt. We both agreed that this conversation could not occur with any black person over the age of sixty who may have once changed our diapers. "I ain't trying to walk up into my grandmama's house talking 'bout, 'Ain't no Jesus.' Nope, not gon' do it," my friend joked. We envisioned the conversation going exactly as it had for this man who had been lovingly corrected while sentenced to eternal damnation.

For another man on the panel, his admittance that he

was a nonbeliever resulted in the dissolution of a romantic relationship. His live-in girlfriend was a backsliding Seventh Day Adventist when they courted and became serious. The more she pressed him about his own religious upbringing, the more he had to admit to himself and to her that he'd never believed in what he sang in church. Although he had fond memories of being a good little Baptist boy, he had stopped going to Sunday service because he'd realized he did not believe the Bible was a book written by god. He thought it deserved no greater placement on the hierarchy of holy books than any others written by people who, though they had some good things to say, had some twisted views that they tried to pin on a supernatural deity who wanted their biases to be mandates for mankind.

"The more I refused to pretend I was convertible, the more fundamentalist she became," the panelist says in the video. He describes his ex-girlfriend going from just keeping the Sabbath to "not wearing pants and not allowing me to watch television on a Friday night—even when I would go to a different side of the house so it didn't interfere with her worship." While he explained that he knew such a wide gap in their worldview would lead to a breakup, my mind stayed on the image of his woman becoming more rigid in her religious practice the more he became honest about his nonbelief.

It could be that she developed a stronger belief in her own faith and recommitted herself to it by being involved with a man that had no place in his life for any faith. Perhaps this nonbeliever's ex would say their relationship was the devil's way of testing her, or god's way of speaking to her heart and reminding her that she had strayed from his path and needed to find her way back.

What I see in her request that he stop watching television until the sun set on Saturday night is a member of our tribe telling this Judas he needed to change his vote. Break open that ballot box and scratch out the name of his wasted write-in candidate. Check the box that made him easier to explain to her family and friends. I see someone he loved saying what the other panelist's grandmother had said to him: "You are being silly with this belief in no one but yourself. Stop it now."

I am not concerned about who is more right. It is not my goal to hold up nonbelievers' logic against believers' faith and declare that those of us who base our hopes on things seen are the uncontested winners in the evolved humanity playoffs. What keeps coming back to me when I listen to the stories of nonbelievers is the image of me mumbling *nam myoho renge kyo* within earshot of my mother, harboring a real sense of fear that I had betrayed . . . something.

No one has ever said to me or other nonbelievers, "We, the black people of the world, believe in this savior god and his son as our only spiritual truth."

No one has had to.

What people whose lives fit into the dominant narrative often do not acknowledge are the many ways in which those of us who are unsuccessful at stuffing ourselves into that narrative are reminded we can lose so much if we don't tuck our legs in further, squeeze that belly in tighter, and fold our entire being into the box that everyone claims is not there while proclaiming its nonexistent presence is the best place for us.

(Everyone else is in here, too! Come on, just suck that gut in a wee bit more!)

I hear black members of The Soka Gakkai International vocalize this loss more than any other demographic of people who find their way to this organization after leaving the religion of their families. It is a kind of a loss that is difficult to quantify in much the same way that women whose husbands occasionally curse them out and call them worthless do not fill up the beds in domestic violence shelters as much as the wives with busted lips and fractured skulls do.

Nichiren Buddhist practitioners of African descent don't speak of being banished. They don't speak of being shamed or scorned because they have found spiritual solace in a faith many of their family and friends associate with every other demographic of people besides Black American ones.

The reminder that they have voted themselves outside of the tribe and therefore have earned its suspicion is not delivered by way of overt and harsh proselytizing. The message is sent when everyone at the table looks at them not bowing their heads when it is time to say grace. If these members are lucky, all they will get is a *who-she-think-she-is* look. If it is an unlucky Thanksgiving, they will get a lecture on respect and not making the holiday all about them. The proselytizing is embedded in the meme that shows up in their inbox on Facebook, sent by a relative who has been made aware of their rejection of the god being many times yet still urges them to "send this to twelve other people who believe Jesus is Lord!" If they are lucky, their "I told you I don't believe Jesus is Lord at Auntie Grace's birthday last week and at Gert's wedding last year" will only be met with silence. If fortune has failed them, there will be half a dozen more Jesus-is-Lord memes by week's end.

It is in the continued assertion that the spiritual practice that has guided their every step and taught them the skills to create their own happiness cannot be considered a spiritual practice at all because it is not based on the worship of *any* deity. It is in the declaration that since their "religion" does not call for the worship of a god, they must be worshipping the devil.

These are not great burdens in the lives of Gakkai members and other humanists who have not subscribed to alternate spiritual practices after realizing they did not believe in god. These slights place somewhere above "Minor Inconveniences of Being a Member of a Tribe" and well beneath "Completely Toxic Interactions that Will Cause Me to Cut Off the Entire Tribe"; they're on par with Netflix not working because you forgot to update your debit card information. They are harmless incidents of petty bullying that will be forgotten by the perpetrator and the victim immediately after they have occurred.

The issue with these minor inconveniences lies in how often they cause nonbelievers to question themselves. If all I have to do is claim belief in this illogical fallacy in order to continue to have access to this tribe, then why don't I just practice my faux-belief like everybody else? More dehumanizing compromise is required of me outside this circle of people who look like me and will have my back when the world reminds me that I am not one of them. Am I becoming too much like the culture I will never trust by rejecting the core belief of the people who will always feel the most like home?

This is the reason nonbelievers like Ayanna Watson start online support groups for other nonbelievers. Seven years ago, she created a page on Facebook called Black Atheists of America simply because she wanted others like her to know there were others like them.

"The vocal and visible atheist groups are still predominantly white, upper-class men," Ayanna said. "And like a lot of white, middle-class American men, their knowledge of the needs of the black community is as limited as their interest in addressing those needs."

Seven years later, 10,000 people are members of this page and the group is a nonprofit organization that has sponsored projects seeking to minister to the disenfranchised in similar ways that the black church has had generations of a head-start doing.

"People still message me privately to say they want to like the page or join the group but they are afraid certain friends and family will notice and they don't want to be bothered with having to explain themselves," Ayanna tells me.

It is not surprising that our fellow nonbelievers choose not to do something as passive as like a Facebook page because they want to avoid the scolding that would follow.

"When I first started the page, it was not uncommon for theists to come onto it and quote Bible verses and rant on about all of us bowing down to Christ during the rapture," Ayanna adds.

Even though she had not started BAA as an invitation to debate the validity of disbelief, members of the tribe still tried to bully her. But she remained true to her original mission: to give black atheists a place where they could confess to their own nonbelief without feeling like freaks and unite with one another to service their community in the same ways that college Greek organizations and, yes, many black churches have done for generations.

Whenever I think I am being too analytical about this— the idea that by rejecting the Christian church and its god construct I am rejecting the social safety net of a people I love—I find myself in a situation where I am reminded I am akin to that third-party voter who many believe is not respecting the hard-won right of my ancestors to cast the ballot.

I call on the name of Jesus on my social media platforms. Social media has made it a preference to communicate through sarcastic clapbacks and clever memes. Using phrases from the black vernacular to emphasis a point includes the common call-and-response heard in black churches, as well as black slang and song lyrics. So, when I start a post on Facebook with "Asian (or African) Jesus," the black folk on my page get the joke. "Fix it, Jesus," as I mentioned earlier, is not an uncommon refrain from the devout in trouble searching for rescue, or for the religious indifferent who find calling on this spirit a familiar way to voice frustration.

I started off a complaint about the aggressive involvement of the parents at the expensive boarding school where I teach in China with, "Dear Asian Jesus, I try so hard to live my life with integrity." I went on to explain how my student's father had been following me around a teacher appreciation dinner trying to bribe me with a leather jacket. The comments on that thread ranged from memes depicting the awkwardness of my situation to requests to accept the jacket and "send it to me." Then I received a direct message from a new friend who asked me to stop saying "Asian Jesus." Since we had become friends in real life several months prior, I assumed she had heard me call on the Christian's symbol of salvation in jest at least half a dozen times.

"I know you don't have to stop saying it," the message read. "I just thought I would ask nicely." When questioned about what exactly bothered her, she said it was hard for her to hear me joke with Jesus's name. "It's a Christian thing." She added a smiley face to soften what could be taken by her new friend as a dogmatic dictate to cease and desist with taking the Lord's name in vain.

It struck me that there are probably several others following my posts who feel the use of this phrase is disrespectful. There are so many others who believe this Jesus person is greater than any other human who has done exactly what he did: fight for the disenfranchised and serve the poor, and later get murdered by those in power who feel threatened by him. So, my new friend and I will have several more moments like this one. Moments where my words will reflect those of a person who does not believe she is in debt to Jesus or his father.

"I respect your telling me privately how this impacts your comfort zone," I said, responding with the same measured tone. "But this is not my cross to bear. Your discomfort with my lack of reverence for Jesus is the result of a value system I don't subscribe to."

And with that, the conversation ended. We remained friends on- and offline.

Because I surround myself with critical thinkers and global-minded professionals, I would not expect a friend who is a theist to be so horrified by my atheism that she would disavow friendship with me. However, the could-you-stop-saying-things-that-remind-me-you-are-not-a-believer message makes the point clear: You can be abnormal. You can be different from everyone else. But. You should know it is abnormal. It is different. And you will not be allowed to forget it.

You can vote for Jill Stein, even in a state Hilary has already turned blue before you put your absentee ballot in the mail. I am glad you protested in a responsible manner instead of throwing away your vote like all those people in those swing states. But it was unrealistic—a wasted vote. A benign waste, but a waste nevertheless.

Your vote does not count if it does not align with the candidate that makes the most sense to "all" of us.

5

Gimme That New Religion

never allow anyone to refer to me as the first lady; it's insulting. If I am the first lady, then who is the second? The third? Why am I being hierarchically ranked?"

Kimberly Peeler-Ringer is no good-ole-church-girl fashioned in the way I remember church girls from when I was one myself. She is a theologian, having studied religion at Vanderbilt University, and knows whole scriptures, not just pull quotes. She has studied several versions of biblical text in several languages for several years. She is married to a pastor who heads a church in Nashville, where she has insisted to more than one ole-school church lady to simply refer to her as Kimberly, sister in Christ who happens to be married to the pastor. Kimberly is a progressive Christian who identifies as a feminist. A *Churched Feminist*. This is the name of the blog I happened upon while searching for a certain type of woman I knew had to exist in the Christian church of 2017.

The first post I read on Kimberly's blog was a thoughtful and nuanced analysis of the church's insistence upon convincing women there were only two roles in which they could find their ultimate worth: wife and mother. She criticized this sexist rhetoric, which happens to be pervasive in the black church.

It has never been a secret that the demographic that is the most faithful in church involvement and the most consistent in its financial support is black women, many of whom are unmarried, some of whom do not have children for any number of reasons. With this in mind, Kimberly called the church's twisted "theology" ridiculous and impractical and insisted that the women who are literally keeping the doors of the church open would not continue to be condescended to; the church was alienating the only base it had left. And they were doing so in the absence of sound scriptural evidence. Wasn't Jesus himself unmarried and childless? Perhaps this was why he had the time, energy, and patience to save the world from sin.

I left the church before I knew what to call the woman I was becoming. Before I was even twenty years old, I had a vague understanding that the black church had stopped filling a need I thought I had and was more of a habit I had formed throughout childhood. Coming from a fundamentalist background and having attended a Seventh Day Adventist school most of my young life, I did not have the language to articulate my dissatisfaction with whatever it was this entity was supposed to give me. But I knew I was a young woman who did not worship matrimony and would not burden myself with submission to a husband. I knew I was a sexually curious young person who found it insulting that my expression of this sexuality should be shamed and put on a leash because a being other than me—the owner of this body, the controller of this expression—said so. The constant attempts to paint my purity as some sort of testament to my closeness to this god being was, in my still-inadequate vocabulary, "a crazy, fucked up mind fuck."

Leaving the insular bubble of my tiny church school and going to the worst public high school in New Orleans was, if I am to give him credit, truly a blessing from the god being. I was sixteen years old when I switched schools and lost interest in church. I am sure many of the other students in this Southern public school full of black people went to church and professed belief in god. However, the fact that it was secular and absent of subtle shaming and indoctrination gave me the space to realize I did not like "the church," even though some of the people who made up the church were likable enough.

I found myself annoyed with the notion that this god being didn't approve of my favorite uncle, my savior at school who routinely read to filth the other boys who teased me, and the choir director who played the piano every week because they expressed their sexuality with other men. Even the backhanded way God's church comforted these sinners bothered me. "God hates the sin, not the sinner," Pastor would say, and then he'd spend a third of his sermon chastising these sinners more harshly than the ones who sinned with women (and sometimes created children these women ended up raising by themselves). Amidst the "Amens" and "Preach it, Passas!" I found myself thinking, *Such a shitty way to say, "It's not you, it's—well, it's just the stuff you do that makes you you . . . that is where the problem lies."* The level of mind fucking was so high I wondered how any of us who eventually left managed to make it out without extensive therapy for years afterward.

Using "because the Bible says" as a reason for isolating entire groups of people as well as a rationale for conforming to an expectation that felt wrong even to the conformist frustrated me the older I got. The supposed values the church held also struck me as impossible to live up to since I believed these mocked anyone who believed the world was bigger than what was written in the Christian holy book, and the interpretations of this holy book were incongruent with who I was at my core.

At nineteen, I didn't know I was a feminist. I just knew this constant refusal to allow women to live their full humanity in God's church was dumb. I didn't know I could label myself a progressive. I just thought it silly and downright hypocritical for this god being to judge good people who did good things based on who they slept with and whether they had engaged in the pleasure of the flesh before a legal marriage occurred.

And now here I was, years later, chatting with Kimberly about being the woman she was and still identifying as a Christian and practicing her faith within the church. Although she has the credentials, Kimberly has never pursued a path to the pulpit. She does not feel called to lead a congregation but to show her sisters in faith that they don't have to be this biblical model of virginal purity and subservient wife that the church continues to uphold as "the standard" for any woman who purports to be a follower of Christ and a serious member of his church. She finds ways to empower women in whom she sees the potential for church leadership. She mentors and leads workshops, strengthening their foundation in the scriptures that are often used—incorrectly—to devalue women and diminish their power.

"Many of these women tell me they are afraid to pursue the pulpit—to be ordained ministers—because if they do, that lessens their chance to get a husband," Kimberly tells me.

It is beyond my realm of understanding to grasp this fear. So, you get the call to minister. You answer that call, devoting yourself to the disciples of Christ who need you to encourage and inspire them to lead lives that will attract others to the word of Christ. There are men who see you take on the call of a god they, too, claim to serve and instead of being attracted to you, they avoid you? They consider you unworthy of partnership? You, who leads an entire congregation? And you are upset that these potential suitors might not shackle you to their mediocre manhood for an entire lifetime? Nope, I can't wrap my brain around it.

While there are a growing number of women who are challenging the patriarchal ideology that male leadership passes off as theology, these women are still the products of generations of marriage being deified and motherhood being framed as synonymous to womanhood. They are not immune to the shame that religious (and secular) institutions project onto women whose power does not come from being chosen by a man or giving birth to a child.

"The way the church teaches wifedom," Kimberly says, "is the equivalent of being a patriarchal assistant."

So those faithful, dynamic women whom Kimberly is training in church leadership are not just fighting against the indoctrination that no matter how much greatness they can achieve for the will of Christ, they must consider how those achievements will impact the fragile egos of the men who might grant them the privilege of wifedom—they are also fighting against the construct of how a woman leads in god's church. She can be the head of the usher board. She can share a special testimony on Women's Day. Pastor might even give up his special seat in the center of the dais for that Sunday when the church's mother gets five minutes to offer words of guidance to the other women struggling to remain faithful and committed to their ultimate goal of salvation.

But to be the official leader of the entire flock seven days a week. To deliver messages that inspired, corrected, and taught hundreds of people. To be the one that counseled married couples, wayward youth, lonely seniors. To. Be. The. Decisionmaker. To be the one who decided the trajectory of the church and how its mission would be carried out over the course of her leadership. Absolutely not. Kimberly's mentees were saying much more than even they were aware of when they admitted: "If I become the pastor, then that one single brother I see every Sunday morning who is god-fearing and ready for a wife won't even consider asking me for a cup of coffee, let alone my hand in marriage."

Hortense, the elderly Jamaican character in Zadie Smith's premiere novel, *White Teeth*, exemplifies a woman who understands and accepts her place in God's church. Hortense's sixteen-year-old granddaughter, Irie, comes to stay with her after a heated argument with Hortense's daughter. Irie, a non-religious possible atheist, is intrigued by her grandmother's fanaticism as a Jehovah's Witness. She is entertained by the drama of her grandmother's fervor. Hortense's calculations of when Judgment Day might arrive and how she can make sure she has moved back to Jamaica when it happens because who wants to meet the Lord in this sinning cesspool of London? Her shouts of praise when her fellow church member, Ryan, shares his ignorant, illogical interpretations of scripture. For an only child who has spent her entire life in a house in which god is a vague idea with parents whose marriage of convenience has turned them into cordial roommates, the extra-ness of her grandmother and Ryan's fanaticism makes her feel like she's living in a bad movie. Watching a bad movie is boring. Living in one makes life more interesting. Irie is quietly amused in ways she never was at home.

What Irie cannot find entertaining, however, is Ryan's dismissal of her grandmother's service to him as a leader in the church. Hortense transcribes Ryan's thoughts onto paper and edits them before they are submitted to church officials. She silences herself when Ryan chastises her for reading the word of god on her own and then questioning him when he explains why her female mind cannot possibly process all the heavy concepts contained within the scriptures. From encouraging Ryan to pursue a higher leadership position in the church to proofreading, typing, and submitting his words to the church's publication, Hortense serves as Ryan's assistant in the ministry, even though she is several decades older than him and has shown through her extreme piety and gleeful suffering that she is committed to the doctrines of the church and is set on being one of the 144,000 chosen on Judgment Day. When Irie expresses her frustration with the way Ryan treats her grandmother, Hortense tells Irie she is taking shit from Ryan now because once she is in god's kingdom, the man in charge of this heavenly prison will listen to her and allow her to lead.

"I know my heavenly father is not like these earthly men," she reassures young Irie. "I will do what I have to do now, but things will be better for the faithful women who are in Heaven."

In short, Hortense makes peace with being treated as an incompetent child because it is not worth the fight to assert her intelligence, to challenge the men who believe their penises are the only credentials they need to grant them speaking rights in Kingdom Hall. She clings to this supernatural man who, for some odd reason, she believes to be more progressive and forward-thinking than the human men whom she has allowed dominion over her religious life.

Although a fictional character, Hortense's underlying acceptance of second-class citizenship is an accurate portrayal of the conservative values of many women who, in the twenty-first century, still believe their silence is but a small price to pay for the overall good of pleasing the supernatural male who, like the human ones who lead his church, only has their best interest in mind. Women who are committed to their faith and who have built their critical thinking muscles through years of academic study and problem solving all admit the church privileges male egos over female labor and shrug their shoulders. "It's natural for a man to lead," they say. "Women do important work too. Does it really matter if it's in the background and we don't get to be out front as much as men?"

This entrenched pathology that women were created as

men's subordinates has bothered women like Kinitra Brown for years. Kinitra, like Kimberly, is an academic—one who uses her university classes to dissect feminist themes in Beyoncé's music and the sexist rhetoric perpetuated in many horror films. She is a scholar and professor who has shaken up the syllabus at the University of Texas at San Antonio with her analyses of pop culture and the societal norms it creates. She, too, considers herself a Christian who believes in salvation through Christ. She, too, has struggled with the trauma the church has inflicted on her as a black woman who thinks it natural to want to assert her power.

"Women can do all of this other shit, but we can't walk across the fucking podium?" Kinitra remembers being about thirteen years old when she asked this in response to being told why, during a certain religious ceremony, it was only the men who would be allowed to take the dais and receive special blessings. She doesn't remember the specifics of the ceremony, but she does remember being infuriated at the suggestion that the women she saw doing all the heavy lifting were less worthy of these privileges than the male leadership. Today, as an adult, she credits her formative years in the black church for preparing her for the research and questioning skills she would later use in pursuing her doctorate degree. She insists she learned to see and appreciate the power of women every Sunday, but "I loathed how I saw them also limiting themselves because they were in the church."

Unlike Kimberly, Kinitra is not as involved in the church today. She did not focus her doctoral studies on Christ and his teachings. Although she still finds value in the calmness of worship and the power of praise, she does not talk about attending any formal church service regularly. In our conversation, I am convinced that she is the most aligned with me in that, although she hasn't "left" the church, the misogyny and homophobia that run rampant through many churches have not been dismantled enough for her to navigate those harmful waters just to get the peace of worship and uplift of praise. "I know you say the New Hope Church of today is not the New Hope of my youth," she told her mother once when she was visiting home and passed on a chance to go to church. "But New Hope ain't changed enough for me yet to go back and deal with the foolishness."

Why do so many people, especially black women, keep going back? I know there are many conservative women in the church who don't feel oppressed by the dogma of "your husband is the head and you are the neck." The opposite of Kinitra and Kimberly are women like my friend Tameka, who does not bat an eye when I suggest the partnership the church upholds as godly sounds more like a parent-child relationship than a marriage between two adults.

"As long as my future husband will lead me correctly according to god's word," she said. "Then it doesn't matter whether it is parent-child or adult-adult. I will submit if he is a real Boaz."

People gon' believe what people gon' believe. If there are women who truly believe their place should be behind men —the ones they marry and the ones they call Pastor—then it is not worth my time nor is it my place to suggest they are misguided. However, this belief does continue to uphold the patriarchal blockades that stand in the way of progress. It does not take a scholar to see the connection between the women-must-merely-assist-the-men rhetoric and the sin-is-sin-but-homosexual-sin-is-far-worse-then-heterosexual-sin hypocrisy. For the Tamekas of the church, who are unbothered by being told regression to their fourteen-year-old self is the Christ-like way to be a wife, I am sure it is even easier to overlook the vitriol that is spouted at anyone who is not heterosexual.

Women like Kinitra are different, however. We both know the basis of the homophobia in the black church is not a scriptural but a patriarchal one. Men benefit a great deal from the strict gender roles that heteronormative spaces enforce. Heterosexual men are assumed to be the prototype for manliness, which is the default setting for ruler. Women, by virtue of their femaleness, are less qualified for this default setting. So, yes, that "funny" musical director who switches and sways a bit too much while leading the choir is inferior, because he is showing a breakdown in his manliness. He is exhibiting the characteristics of a woman and having sex with men. When those man-looking ladies who come to church in pants and wearing no makeup eschew their femaleness, they are trying to reverse the natural order of things. They are trying to embody the default setting when God has not given them a penis.

Why does Kinitra bother to call herself a Christian? Why does she join, even on occasion, this gathering of people who believe that to behave in ways that suggest we are living in the twenty-first century is to go against the edict of god?

"It's sort of like when you love something so much, you want to try your best to improve that thing *because* it means so much to you," she explains. And that is the thing: for progressive Christians, the love of god and salvation through his son are core values. It is the belief in that founding principle of Christianity that binds progressives to conservatives. It is quite simple for me to walk away from the misogyny because I don't get that peaceful calm from worshipping god as Kinitra does. I don't believe in him in the way she does. I cannot reconcile the demonization of queer brothers and sisters with the contentment that I am also being encouraged weekly on my journey to salvation through Jesus. I don't see Jesus Christ as any different from Martin Luther King, Jr. He, too, stood up for those who could not stand up for themselves and was murdered. So remaining silent or trying to educate through scriptural knowledge those who shamed queer members all the while taking advantage of their talents had no appeal to me. There never was and continues to be no payoff for me to listen to and challenge sexist and homophobic rhetoric for the sake of exacting change in the church.

People like Kimberly are doing difficult work that only they can do. If you love something enough, shaping it into something even more lovable is a natural desire. Honorable, even. And there are women in these churches doing just that. Kimberly informs me that for those women who do take on the role of real leadership, it can be exhausting. There are usually only one or two of them in any given church and young female pastors are often expected to espouse a desire to become wives without actually dating their single counterparts.

When she was first licensed in the ministry, Kimberly saw a stark difference in how much help the young male pastors received in the dating game as opposed to her and the other women. "People would invite the male pastors over to their house for dinner to meet their niece or tell them about a smart single lady who they talked to, offering to get her number for them," she says. But no one offered to introduce Kimberly and her girlfriends to eligible single men. It was as if although they were well into their late twenties and early thirties, they were expected to be chaste single ladies yet somehow also become godly wives by the time they were offered a chance at the pulpit. And often, these women needed the distraction of romantic euphoria much more than the male pastors. When you are the only woman in a leadership role, ALL the women in the church are your ministry. So the struggles in which these women find themselves become part of your service expectations as well as the normal duties required of church leaders.

MY PRACTICE AS A NICHIREN BUDDHIST HAS contributed a great deal to my evolution as a human being. Years before I discovered it, I was sort of bouncing around, disconnected from any real spiritual core. I can now credit my formative years in the church for making a life principle clear to me: a connection to a spiritual practice higher than my own desires is key to my feeling a sense of centeredness and peace. For the ten or fifteen years when I claimed belief in atheism and/or agnosticism, I sensed simply professing nonbelief in a Western version of faith was not enough to truly feed my soul and give me a sense of mission beyond being kind to other humans. While the ideal of love is at the core of all spiritual teachings around the globe, spiritual work requires more than mouthing peace and love (as a trite greeting more than an actual wish for someone's life). There is a reason why those who do more than vocalize a desire to be fit become more fit. Lifting weights and eating a semi-healthy diet will not get you the same health outcome as the person who has a regular, rigorous exercise regimen and a consistent habit of eating whole foods prepared at home. The same exists in spirituality. It is a practice. A training. A journey. Just like becoming an adult, a working professional, a writer, a spouse. You must put in work alongside others who are doing the same type of work as you for it to add benefit to your life.

My Buddhist practice has made me more understanding of Christians and why the faithful still practice with the church even when they don't necessarily believe in the harmful interpretations of Christ's teachings that his followers wrote centuries ago. While people use the terms religion and faith and spirituality interchangeably, I don't see value in dissecting what each term connotes in theory and in day-to-day practicality. I will use the word "faith" for the sake of focus. It is greater than the organized entities we align ourselves with when we claim belief in a spiritual teaching. It is what is at the center of spirituality and the seed from which the desire to begin a spiritual practice grows. So it seems the more precise word.

While talking to Kimberly and Kinitra about their faith and why they need it, I found myself wondering why any of us bother. In my spiritual practice alone, it is nearly impossible to be a slacker. My practice puts the onus of my life and its development on my shoulders. I cannot afford to be a backsliding Buddhist. My life is tied to what I put into my spiritual work. It requires a level of commitment to the world and its inhabitants that also makes it difficult to practice with anything other than an all-or-nothing attitude. So when I wondered why Kinitra bothered calling herself a Christian, I was questioning why I continue to commit to the rigorous work of chanting twice daily, studying my mentor's guidance, and challenging myself to find the solution to my problems where the problems begin: with me.

Kimberly devotes time not only to her own growth as a Christian but that of her sisters. She is committed to getting them to ally with her as they create a church Jesus Christ himself would be eager to attend. A church that embraces the people he loved without judgment, asking nothing of them but that they hold up the faithful among them.

What is the benefit of such work? It is the same benefit one gets from faith itself. Here is the truth we all learn even before the ink on our overpriced college diplomas has dried. If you let it, Life will catch you off guard in an alleyway and beat you like you stole its woman, leaving you paralyzed and damn near dead. Faith, as its most basic function, exists to help make such ass whippings more palatable. Gives you the extra breath to call out to that passerby who would never even have turned her eye to the dim alley had she not heard this faint little whisper. Faith, regardless of the religion one might subscribe to, is what makes the harshness of humanity easier to navigate. It is what makes a commitment to other humans worth the effort, even amidst the cruelty of humanity itself.

So of course progressive women feel the Christian church is a good spiritual fit for them. When Life went at their head with that steel bat, Christianity did what Buddhism does. What Islam does. What Hinduism does. What Judaism does. Of course, they can challenge the church's isolation of people who make them uncomfortable while living the fullness of their womanhood without apologies. Their need for relief, for strength is fulfilled within the walls of their chosen church. Though many within those walls have pushed back against the evolution of humankind and the change it brings, this doesn't equate to a loss of faith in the spiritual practice itself.

Even for progressive Christians who are conflicted about the value of the church, the belief in the power of god and his saving grace remain a core value they never question. "For a long time, I hid the fact that I was a Christian," my friend Alisa shares with me. "It felt like a terrorist group even to me." She adds this last part with no sense of irony, no chuckle to soften the analogy. She, a queer woman who believed in a woman's right to terminate a pregnancy as well as her right to agency over all other aspects of her life, should have been the most anti-Christian demagogue if ever there was one.

"I had a deeply religious experience when I was six years old," Alisa explains. And it is this experience that she has come back to as an adult. She doesn't believe much of what happens in church has anything to do with god. It is more akin to people trying to make sense of what doesn't make sense, even though they pretend it all makes perfect sense to them. Yet she still goes to church regularly. She has been accepted into two of the most prestigious seminary programs in the United States and plans to study theological doctrines, just as Kimberly Peeler-Ringer and Kinitra Brooks did.

When Alisa shares this good news with me, I ask if she feels her religious life outside of academia will be as accommodating to her mission of "knowing scripture well enough to defeat homophobes." She says she has no idea what she will do with her divinity degree once she earns it. She knows that she needs to align with a structured program where she can investigate and critique the texts that have served as the foundation of the one book Christians count as the only truth ordained by their god. If she is to be successful at "countering those who created the system that tries to tell us how to think about God or Jesus," she must put in the work, both spiritual and intellectual.

I believe religion serves an important role in the twenty-first century regardless of the doctrine on which religious teaching is based, and that this role can be fulfilled even given the potential for abusive implementation of those teachings by self-serving religious "authorities." Faith and its practice are necessary, despite the lack of scientific data to provide "proof" of its truth. The mere fact that so many people subscribe to belief in something is overwhelming evidence that despite many valid reasons to do otherwise, humans have hope. They believe in something they cannot explain. They look for a spiritual belief structure to order their lives and give it meaning beyond the accumulation of things and people. It is this desire to latch onto goodness—the potential for it in themselves and the deity from which they believe goodness originates—that I believe those of us committed to humanity must capitalize on and use as a tool for continued evolution.

Caveat: The content of the following paragraph is not

based on months of research and data gleaned from multiple, cross-referenced sources. It is based solely on my observations of and conversations with people over the last decade or so.

Many of us want something "new" in our spiritual belief structure. Alisa has criticized desperate churches' attempts at "new" when they hire young, hoodie-wearing pastors and have special hip-hop services that they believe will entice disenchanted youth back to the pews. "I know they mean well," she says, "but adding strobe lights and installing a new sound system doesn't turn your parents' basement into a nightclub that people will wait in line to get into." She thinks church leaders show how clueless they are when they are confused why this way of being "new" doesn't keep its target demographic past a few services.

The fact is, this is not the new that most of us—young and old—seek. We want a new that does not tell us we are unworthy. We want a new that does not expect us to believe this god being is so petty that he is unfriending our gay college roommate (not because of what he posts but because of what he *says* when he posts) and raining down calamities on countries that support the twentieth-century ideal of women having agency over their own bodies, autonomy in their life choices.

We want a new that mirrors the complexity of the human experience in a time period where the word "family" does not necessarily signify the rearing of children by a man and a woman who have signed legal paperwork to formalize their relationship. We want a new that offers a practical prototype for basking in the beauty of this earthly home and not waiting for the possibility of a heavenly one. We want a new that does not concern itself with how much we can and cannot conform to what the god being has dictated, but how much we can create lives of absolute happiness. A new that holds us accountable for supporting someone else in creating their version of authentic joy.

We want a new that reminds us we are enough, not offering guilt for already believing we are.

When Alisa says she is choosing to leave her career as an educator to pursue theological study that defeats those who continue to use patriarchal interpretations of scriptures to "lovingly" shame the non-heterosexual, she is saying, "I want a church where I am enough. I do not need to atone for being who I am." She may not say those exact words, but her commitment to studying the scriptures and the context in which they were written speak of a necessity for a religion that is based on individuals' willingness to critique texts that are used to perpetuate human misery. A religion that does not encourage its followers to rely on discomfort draped in Bible-speak to justify judging people whose only sin seems to be that they have the audacity to live outside a narrative of normal that has not been the only version for at least forty years.

When Kimberly rebukes the prestige well-meaning church members ascribe to the female Christian who happens to marry the male leader of the church, she is saying to those believers: "I don't need to be the first and you don't need to be the second. Neither of us need to be ladies, either. I didn't need to marry power to know my own."

If there is any demographic of Christian who needs this new more, it is the devoted, sacrifice-addicted black women who have been the most manipulated by the old. The sense of relief I feel when I talk to progressive black women who do not back down in the face of generations' worth of theologies that damn them for believing they are enough and wanting to be treated as if they are is indescribable. The black church will be forced to expedite its evolution once black women realize that the cute consolation prizes of patriarchy are paltry trinkets when held up against the rewards of liberty from the expectation to shrink yourself.

The new is on its way. If you were to ask Kimberly, Kinitra, and Alisa, they would probably say the new has been here. Those who stayed when I left have been building it for decades now.

6

Wherever You Go,
There You Are

$\mathcal{I}$t starts as a whisper. A faint voice as you slosh through snow on a cold January morning, hoping the train is running only a little late because you scheduled a parent meeting before first period on this Monday morning during the cruelest portion of the greedy winter season. The voice from somewhere in your conscious asks questions like, "What else?" and "Why here?" These questions are muffled by the familiar screech of late trains sliding into stations and aggravated commuters cussing while side-eyeing each other for taking up too much space in the car they will all share for the next twenty minutes.

There are other questions, too. *Is this enough? Could there be more? Am I too comfortable?* These thoughts flash quickly across your consciousness when you turn over and kiss the man you love good night. The warmth of love and contentment of partnership overpower these questions you are not even sure you hear.

You find yourself thinking all this when you are joking with coworkers about that magical thing the latest education reformer insisted you must do to save your students that you didn't bother to do and your students seemed to learn despite being unsaved. But the flashes of faint questions never last long. You teach a good lesson—one where the kids listen for at least half the class and produce some sort of evidence that they have learned something close to what you intended. In the two seconds it takes you to grapple with which student to call on to respond to your question, you found yourself wondering, *Am I too comfortable?* You choose an unsuspecting student whose shaky voice as she stumbles through her response drowns out the thought about being too comfortable you're not even sure you had.

You sit at brunch with women who adore you almost as much as you adore them and in the midst of your bottomless mimosa haze, there are cloudy words floating about, already starting to dissipate and turn back into air: "But what if there is more than this?"

There are many people who are running away. Women who have endured years of marriages that have flattened them only to be dumped by the men who had ironed them out. Young people who never found themselves in college and want to hide away in another country where people won't badger them with, "So, what are you doing next?" Men whose average looks and bland personalities transform into handsomeness and worldliness upon setting foot into countries where beautiful women unruined by feminism are plentiful.

What about those of us who were running toward something? Those of us who had full, joyous lives that we had carefully created and could have continued to enjoy if they had remained as they were? What causes us to uproot those lives? What is it that makes us say, "I love my life here, but I am moving it there."

In conversations with other expats, it becomes clear to me that they, too, heard the whisper: "It's like I could see myself being *that* teacher. The one who taught in the same school in the same district, heck, even in the same room, for like thirty years."

For Sabrina, a divorced mother in her forties, what most people would relish in the security of a reliable job felt like the easy way out to her. She had been preparing middle school students for high school for a decade. She knew and loved her students. She had a supportive and appreciative administration who respected her work. She also had family and friends who shared her values. There was never a deficit of people in her and her son's life. From her ex-husband to her second cousin, Sabrina knew the people who made up her community were there because they wanted to be and all were the better for it.

A charmed life. An adulthood done right.

But. "I knew there were other places in the world that could offer me the same quality of life and even better, since I grew up with military parents and had lived in different countries," Sabrina says. She talks about feeling like she was shortchanging her son by staying in the North Carolina town where her parents had grown up and eventually settled back into when Sabrina was heading to college. "In the twenty-first century, was it really in his best interest to keep my son in this small bubble where he never had to fend for himself and never even had to question why everyone around him believed certain things, never had to be proven wrong about his own assumptions? He was too sheltered and I was too comfortable."

A woman with an advanced degree and a fifteen-year work history does not have to worry if she will "make it" in whatever country she chooses to start anew. When her field is education and she has excelled in that field, she will not be putting her meager belongings into a backpack and catching the cheapest flight to her destination, having no idea how things will work out once she sets foot onto this foreign soil with only an extended tourist visa and fantastical dreams.

She will be offered an attractive salary and benefits package at a private school that comes with housing and reduced, if not free, tuition for her child. She will be sponsored for a work visa and will not have to take on the complicated application process alone. Her employer will streamline the process so well that when other newcomers to the country ask for her advice on an issue they are having with their own visa, she will be flummoxed. She will not be able to offer any guidance, as she will have no idea how the documents she submitted to HR turned into the document on her passport that grants her legal residence in this country.

What exactly is it that GROWN women with GROWN women lives are looking for when they say they are moving abroad because they are "too comfortable?" For the twenty-something backpacker, discomfort is exactly what they get when they throw caution to the wind. They do have college degrees, but they don't have a work history or network of colleagues and resources in their field. So in many ways they are embarking on this "shake things up" mission without a safety net, pretty much begging for crappy living spaces, placeholder jobs, and just enough income to live decently in regions of the world with lower costs of living. They also have no mortgages, no aging parents, no proximity to retirement to understand the need to plan for it.

That word, "discomfort," translates for many as "financial hardship that builds character." But when you move abroad as an experienced professional with US citizenship, your life is likely to become more privileged, more "comfortable" than when you lived in the United States.

Perhaps a better word is *challenge*. Sabrina and I were looking for a challenge.

Some years had passed since we had overcome those first few years in the classroom when you feel like that expensive-ass degree taught you nothing about how to educate American teenagers in an effective and humane manner. We had taken on other roles besides English teacher, mentoring those starting out in the profession, earning an administrative credential, learning different curricula, even developing our own. We had bought property. We had traveling experiences that ranged from "for entertainment purposes only" to "life transformation and rejuvenation" to "change the world one mission trip at a time." We had loved and lost. Yes, we had enjoyed the deliciousness of a Ralph Angel we never saw a future with anyway and uplifted the baes who could have been husbands if only they didn't _____ or we had _____ or both of us had been better at _____.

We felt the softness in our legs. The mushiness that once was muscle reminding us that we had plateaued.

"I could have stayed in North Carolina for years. It was a good life. I had my family all around me." Sabrina pauses as she tries to explain the why. If she were happy with her life, then why uproot it and move it half way around the world? She was still an English teacher. Now her son's friendship circle encompassed the children of rich, privileged expats like herself, sprinkled in with a few "local" kids whose lives so resembled those of their foreign schoolmates that they dreaded school-sponsored interactions with "real" locals while their classmates looked forward to them.

Sabrina and I have been having this conversation since we became friends. We were not part of the local community and by no stretch of the imagination could we claim to have been transformed by these people whose country we had invaded with our blue passports and native-speaking English. We did have more opportunities to advance in our professional careers because of our Western privilege. The color of our passport made up in many ways for the color of our skin. White colleagues still carry their privilege with them overseas and the deference to their supremacy cannot be dismissed. However, Sabrina and I were aware the only thing that delivered us from the questions of parents who wanted the best teachers for their children were the buzzwords we had intentionally written into our faculty bios: *graduate degree from New York University; taught American curriculum, including Advanced Placement; adjunct professor at Boston University.*

Amidst our comfortable expat lives, we have felt our muscles tightening again. Daily, we navigate waters that require us to strengthen our stroke or sink into the undercurrent that can pull a swimmer down with a swift sea wave. Yes, there is more time to pursue hobbies such as traveling, brunching, and writing because of all the staff we can hire to deal with the mundane chores of life. Yes, there are more opportunities for advancement in our field and small business ownership. Our money goes much farther. There are also more ways to make money without the red tape one would have to go through in the States.

However, there is also dealing with a new kind of life that would likely never have happened had we stayed in America. And this is where the discomfort/challenge works to force us over that plateau we had hit back home.

Parents often remark that they never knew real love until they had their children. They never knew how important another human being could be to them until they took on the responsibility of raising a child completely dependent on them. I did not need to give birth to learn this lesson in interdependence; I just needed to move to a foreign country alone. For it was this experience that made me work harder to form alliances with other women. Knowing that had I chosen the wrong job to give my passport to or the wrong man to date or the wrong moto-taxi to take could result in my finding myself in a life-altering situation that I could not navigate alone is the sole reason I took my friendships more seriously after going abroad than I ever had when I was still in the country of my birth.

I had no choice but to strengthen my loyalties to the women I decided I wanted in my life. My decision to make myself available to them—to articulate what I too often assumed they already knew—was rooted in this love that we had for each other. In the immediacy of an emergency, we were all we had.

"You do know, you could have waited for me and I would have had your back," I said to a friend in Kigali. She'd just told me this hilarious story of how she locked herself out of her house and didn't have her phone with her so she walked over to my house on the other side of town, thinking that maybe I would be home and . . .

"Yeah," she said. "I don't know how you could have helped me, but I felt like I should just go to your house."

Even though I was not home and did not help her then, I wanted to make sure she knew that her instincts were right. She most definitely could have relied on me, for anything ranging from using my phone to call her landlord to staying at my house until she decided she didn't need to stay there anymore.

I have relied on relative strangers to guide me around countries where I could have vanished off the face of the earth and no one with a connection to me would have been aware of my disappearance for at least seventy-two hours. I have mentally planned the escape routes of young women who have sacrificed their emotional safety, leaving themselves vulnerable to manipulation, because they were afraid and lonely. I have checked in with these women under the guise of "going out" because I knew they could not see the crack and I was waiting for the moment I needed to call their mama and say, "Your daughter is on the next plane back to Philly, she will need a hug when it lands."

I have suffered no financial discomfort. No worries about how I will pay my bills that have kept me up at night. What I have experienced since moving abroad is a need to reassess, to readjust, to identify and acknowledge what I know to be true, even if those truths do not mirror the truths of others.

I HAVE MANAGED TO FALL IN LOVE TWICE IN THE three years I have lived overseas. Although I have been in two different regions of the world for these three years, both of my loves have been passionate West African men. One bae had only left Africa when he moved to Asia and the other bae had only traveled within the continent, venturing out past his own country only once. By West African #2, I had become ever more clear on who I was and who I was not. Who I was: an American woman who, without a doubt, was descended from the continent of Africa. Who I was not: a woman who was interested in upholding the values of African culture that advertised itself as "family-centered" but should be branded as patriarchy peddling.

I remember coming to this conclusion when I narrowly escaped marriage to my Ghanaian boyfriend. We were in the early part of the relationship, where there is little time for argument because all the sex and post-coital confessions of love took up what few hours were left in the day after work. The first time we had a significant disagreement, he announced: I do not want to discuss this anymore, you need to stop talking.

When he turned away from me as if I were a petulant teen who had over stepped her bounds, I felt it my duty to disavow him of the erroneous assumption he had made about the woman he loved. He seemed uncomfortable with my ignoring his edict to shut the hell up, but remained silent as I explained to him he was dating a forty-year-old woman and not a fourteen-year-old child. I would not silence myself because he decided it was too much emotional work to address the conflict we were having.

He listened, although grudgingly, as I continued to state my concerns about our relationship. He presented his and we came to a resolution that I knew would temporarily assuage the problems we were having. As we kissed and made up, I allowed this thought to rest on my mind: *Our love is not long for this world, as this man is a damned fool.*

Throughout my early womanhood, I assumed my ambivalence about marriage was only because there were other things I wanted to do before I actively sought a husband. Then came Nigerian Bae. Through this relationship, I came to accept that I was not just indifferent to marriage; I was disinterested in it. Falling in love with two men who adored me and who were committed to commitment even more than they were committed to me made me be more honest about what I had been claiming was a core belief: I value marriage. My three years abroad have presented me with opportunities to live up to this belief, and each time my choices have shown otherwise.

Sexism aside, Ghanaian Bae was a hardworking man who made me feel protected and loved. He had shown me several times that he was capable of more open-minded ways of coupling that flouted the strict gender roles prevalent in many parts of the continent. During one of the arguments that followed our first major one, he thanked me for telling him exactly why I was angry instead of appeasing him with silence. I could have worked on his mindset even more so over the years—he seemed a willing enough participant—but my life abroad had confirmed that I was more than enough for me. All of those quivering proclamations I had made in my twenties after having read some feministy stuff had now become solid truths. The amazing, purpose-filled life I was not sure I was supposed to even want, let alone accomplish, had become a life I knew existed for me and most other women I encountered.

While love and partnership themselves did not threaten to risk the life I had built, the wrong marriage did. I stood to gain much more from keeping a bae I adored in my life than doing paperwork on a relationship that would cause me to suffer the endless consequences that would come when/if my Bae-turned-Hubby made poor decisions I could not control. I did not fantasize about "building together." I felt already built (and quite well, too).

IN MY THREE YEARS ON TWO DIFFERENT CONTINENTS, I have continued to talk with women who long to meet their husbands in these more traditional countries. The choices these women make support the core belief I admit I do not subscribe to.

I remember an acquaintance in Rwanda filling me in on the interminable process of getting her marriage license. She was marrying a Ugandan man who didn't have a "proper" birth certificate and other legal documents to meet the standards of England, where she needed their marriage to be legally recognized. There were gut-splitting details about having to cross the border into Uganda on her days off from work to talk to a village elder to get some sort of "oral" confirmation of her intended's birth. There were even more hilarious stories of government officials requiring "just one more stamp" on a document she had been told a week before she didn't really need but was now, for some reason, of utmost importance.

"We have the ceremony set for July," she would say, laughing. "But who knows if we will ever be legally married until, like, August . . . if we are lucky."

I chuckled along with her as she vented about this arduous journey to matrimony, thinking to myself, *Hmmm, she really wants to be married, huh?* I had met her fiancé once and he seemed to be a stand-up guy who loved her just as much as she loved him. She was not the only one putting in the legwork to make sure this relationship became legally binding. But it was all this legwork that struck me as the difference between my acquaintance and me. She valued the institution of marriage as much as I valued love. Were I in the same situation, I would not care enough to go through the trouble. Yes, I would inconvenience myself to support the man I loved in a variety of ways. I would change my vacation plans if he were having cash-flow problems and wanted to join me on my next adventure. I would eat humble pie and apologize when I knew I was right if it meant ending an argument that was not worth the discord in our relationship. But crossing borders to recreate birth certificates? Spending copious amounts of hard-earned money to file documents and locate ones that had been misplaced or forgotten?

And this is notwithstanding the obstacles my acquaintance would have to surmount once she became the main wage earner in the household (which would be the case, given her Western privilege). She would go from being a frazzled fiancée to a white, Western wife who controlled the financial destiny of a grown man whose culture had convinced him his penis declared him chief of their matrimonial village. From what I could tell when she talked about him, he was not a slacker and believed in "helping out" around the house. But I knew what men from patriarchal cultures expected of their wives—even in these modern marriages where they allow their wives to work outside the home. She would have to carry a lot; with his "help," of course.

Accepting my ambivalence about marriage has reminded me how much I admire the approach by many Eastern cultures. Years ago, when I was doing a research project in Kolkata, India, I talked to a group of middle-class Bengali women about the still-held practice of arranged marriage. Only one woman in the group of about twelve was in a "love marriage." The others had married the men their parents had selected for them. They seemed indifferent to the choice of mate selection being taken from them. They teased the younger woman in the room who had convinced her parents to allow her to marry the man she was already in love with, but the teasing had a jovial tone devoid of any envy.

The women explained the process by which parents selected mates. There was a consideration of the family from which the young man came. Good parents didn't just consider whether the family had financial means but also if they had the same values and ideals as their own. One woman said her mother ruled out one of her potential suitors because his temperament did not seem a good complement to her daughter's. "He was so dull and unlively," she said. "She knew I needed someone with more . . . just more life."

There was no great amount of consideration given to "romantic chemistry" as we think of it in the West, however. "The first few years of marriage is when you date your husband the way you think of dating in the West," one of the older women explained. "Before the children come, you have time to get to know him and you joke and play with each other. This is when you fall in love."

Even though I was having this conversation years before I was able to admit to myself that marriage was not an institution I desired, I had immense respect for how these women said their culture went about marriage. They approached it as a practical building of a life. Taking the romanticism out of it stripped it down to its most basic function. I have always considered myself a pragmatic romantic, so it was unsurprising to me that these women were content in these marriages that were based on practicality and had learned to grow into the romantic love many Westerners believe is a requirement for a marriage to begin.

I understand the East's arranged marriages formed out of practicality better than I do the West's obsession with doing paperwork for a romantic relationship because you are in love with your partner. When I was on a private tour of Kuala Lumpur, my guide was a charismatic man in his early sixties named Guna. His father had relocated from his homeland in India and had met his mother in Malaysia when they were both young. Guna had grown up in a small town in northern Malaysia but had lived his entire adult life in Kuala Lumpur,

NO THANKS | 119

where he and his wife had raised three children who were all accountants. As we ate lunch, he shared with me the process of finding his youngest child a husband.

"We have hired a matrimonial agent since my daughter is very busy with her job; she does not have the time to meet the young men my wife and I know from our own circle." Guna admitted that the families they had formed alliances with over the years had sons who were not equal to their daughter, which was why they needed to widen the net via a professional matchmaker. "Even doctors who work in public hospitals here are not paid as well as my daughter, who is a manager at a big firm. There needs to be balance in the income, especially if the wife is a high earner." He seemed hopeful because a prospect the matchmaker had located was a surgeon and they generally were paid more than a doctor working in a standard hospital. Guna made no pretense that his daughter, who was knocking on thirty and had established a career with good pay for herself, should have to settle. He thought it naïve and foolish to pretend that a man who earned significantly less than her would be an acceptable partner. For an educated woman with a successful career, he said, marrying a man who had not managed to reach similar heights would cause too much discord throughout the lifetime of a union. "The only time that works is when the wife is not the successful one. It will not work if the wife earns a lot more than the husband."

I listened for Guna's voice to betray a tone of frustration. I expected him to lament his decision to invest in the private school education that instilled a hard work ethic in his daughter, which yielded her expendable income and professional options. But there was not even a subtle tone of remorse. It was fact: his daughter was an accomplished woman, which meant he had to work harder to find her a husband who matched what she brought to the adulthood table.

As Guna shared the near misses he and the matchmaker had encountered in their search, I thought of what I had said to Nigerian Bae when he wondered why I didn't entertain the possibility of marrying him.

"I don't do struggle love, hun," I told him.

He was a loving man who made me feel protected and safe. Yes, he was imperfect, but not in distressing ways that would cause my friends to pull me on the side and ask what the hell was I thinking. The reality, however, was that Nigerian Bae did not enjoy the same privileges my blue passport and American salary granted me. He was not destitute and downtrodden, as many believe is the norm in Africa, but I was able to move more freely around the world and had access to more financial and professional opportunities than he had. To pretend this did not bother me seemed silly. To allow him to believe I wanted to be partnered so badly that I could look beyond how much partnership with him weakened my ability to build a better financial life seemed cruel to him and unfair to me.

So, without much agony, I did what Guna had been doing for the last several years as he searched for a potential suitor for his daughter: I opted out of binding my entire life to a man who was not my financial and professional equal. We could still do the love thang, though. We could carry along with a monogamous relationship in which our physical and emotional needs were met. But if we were to embark on a negotiation regarding the only type of marriage I would be comfortable entering, there were precious few chips with which he could bargain. It was not his fault he was short on chips. It wasn't so much about fault as it was about fact: I had far more than he had and was unwilling to overlook this in order to have a husband who loved me. Several men had loved me up until now. Several had made me feel protected and safe. None had given me a legitimate reason to become their wife. Neither had this one.

There are more than a few extraordinary women who move abroad for professional and personal growth but also are focused on meeting their husbands in the midst of all this "becoming." These women are not the caricatures we see so often on television that we have come to accept such fictional foolishness as fact—the black women who have bought into the fallacy that something is wrong with them and nobody loves them so they get naked for any guy who is nice to them. These are not the well-traveled, well-read, funny, shapely, upwardly mobile sisters who cannot appreciate and enjoy their full lives because their naked ring fingers mock their attempts at successful womanhood and haunt them late into the night.

These are black women who value marriage. Women who are certain the institution will be a part of their destiny, a lifestyle that will suit them well. Women who make choices in their lives that would result in their achieving this goal as they have achieved others.

One of them said to me, "If I don't have more dates with men who are husband-worthy in the next few months, I am not extending my contract. I can go back to London for all this bullshit."

She was a beautiful, kind and accomplished woman of African descent who had accepted a job in Rwanda because she was excited about being involved in its growing economy. She had relocated to Kigali because of the opportunity to work in a different sector than she had been in London and to be involved in the further development of an African nation. But she was also certain she wanted to marry within the next few years. She wanted to have children as well, which needed to happen within the next few years. She had assumed the goal of marriage would be easy enough to reach in a culture where marriage and children were the only true ways to claim adulthood and not have anyone question you.

When she found herself no closer to meeting this goal, staying in Rwanda—a country she had only grown to "like enough"—no longer was useful to her.

She, unlike me, viewed unmarried adulthood as counter to her value system. I was going to leave Rwanda after my contract ended. The lack of potential husbands did not factor into my desire to leave as much as it did for her, though. I did not concern myself much with how the men I met in Kigali were philandering benders of truth. I did not date them when I discovered they were. It frustrated me as a heterosexual woman to have a lack of dating options, but the likelihood that the longer I stayed in Kigali, the longer I would remain unmarried filled me with no more anxiety than the likelihood that I would have to take moto-taxis less often during rainy season and shell out more francs on regular ones.

My reaction to the possibility of remaining single in all the countries in which I would live was similar to my reaction that I would remain a teacher in all the countries in which I would live. I enjoyed being single and I enjoyed teaching, so why would a job as an attorney I would never be offered or the absence of a proposal to embark on a coupling practice I didn't really care about instill any feeling—good or bad—in me?

I don't know if I would have realized my disinterest in being a wife had I still been in New York City. The diversity in coupling practices in my beloved New York makes it difficult to see how your lack of desire for married life is not necessarily odd, but still not the norm. There is a trend in major American cities of downplaying the rite of passage that marriage represents. Admitting my lack of interest in that rite would not have been as challenged as it has been in countries where there is more of a monolithic allegiance to the value of marriage.

Nigerian Bae did not believe an adult relationship could call itself that if it did not have marriage as its ultimate objective. I loved him and was committed to catching planes to see him in Malaysia, where he and his cousin were struggling to get a business off the ground shipping goods to and from Nigeria. When I visited him in Kuala Lumpur, he cooked jollof rice for me and made sure I was safe when I explored the city on my own. He proved himself to be a decent man who thought it his responsibility to make sure I was comfortable in his home.

I still had no desire to be Bae's wife. But I did consider our relationship to be a real one. One in which there was commitment and encouragement and support. When the topic of marriage came up, Bae did make stellar arguments for why society could not continue without the institution of marriage. Those sound arguments did not convince me to consider marrying him, but they did cause me to think about the practical logic behind so many cultures hinging their continuation on this family structure.

I have found myself in the sweet spot of being the woman of a man who was commitment-ready while I was not interested in the commitment for which he had been raised to be ready. There were many advantages of resting cozily in this spot. The greatest was getting the opposite of what women often get in the States when they are of a certain age and dating for a greater purpose than a free meal. Neither Ghanaian Bae nor Nigerian Bae shied away from the "What is this?" conversation. We never really had the conversation, because once we felt a connection, we knew and acknowledged what it was. Although talks of marriage happen too quickly for my American tastes in regions like Africa, I see the fact that they happen as a refreshing reminder that men should want to be held responsible for and accountable to the women they claimed to love.

MY PSEUDO-IMMERSION INTO THESE FOREIGN CULTURES has not transformed any of my core beliefs, but it has forced me to listen as others revealed ideals they held on to as tightly as I did to mine. To reconsider what I believe is the superior way to love, the more enlightened way to live. The number of times I have been the only person in the room disturbed by some "arcane, eighteenth-century belief" is so high I have now trained my face to morph into an un-

moved, nonplussed look that matches my neutral "Oh really?"
tone.

While helping my Chinese colleague celebrate her birthday, I asked how old she was. I began with my standard,
"Now that you are eighteen, you have to be careful about
your choices. Your record is permanent." My colleague responded with a chuckle and, "Oh, eighteen . . . how I wish."
She seemed hesitant to mention her real age. I found that
odd, considering she looked to be in her late twenties.

Later, the coworker did tell me her age. It was the timid
confession of an eighth-grade student who whispers her interest in entering the poetry contest, but only if you read over
her poem first. "I am twenty-nine," she said to me as we were
leaving the home of a fellow coworker where we had all sung
"Happy Birthday" and eaten chocolate cake. "But I am still
unmarried." This confession came with lowered eyes.

I had to think about my response. I had just spent two
years in Rwanda, the most progressive country in Africa
when it came to governmental policies on gender equality
but still attached to its training of girls to believe no matter
what they accomplished, nothing would ever supersede being
a mother and wife.

"Is that a bad thing?" I finally asked.

She quickly nodded. "In China, to be this close to thirty
without a husband . . ." She didn't finish the sentence. Her
voice trailed off and she looked down at the floor again.

"It must be hard for you, I imagine." I paused to see how
much more she wanted to offer.

"I am a single dog."

I had heard of this term before and knew that unmarried

women of her age were called this by friends and family who meant "no harm." The way she assigned herself the title made me wonder if I were more offended by it than she was.

Although I was clear on my core belief about marriage, I reminded myself in this moment that it was more beneficial for us both if I focused on supporting her instead of asserting my own identity. The difference between the two, I was learning, is quite significant. The urge to indoctrinate another is strong. And as an American, this urge to assert my superiority over everyone else is encoded into my DNA. These last three years, I have fought to command my intellectualism to take a backseat to my compassion.

"Well, if you want to be married, I wish you well," I told her. "I hope you find what you need when you need it to have the life you want." I left her with the assurance that when she did marry, she would have had so many precious years alone, a treasure young wives never get the luxury of experiencing. "Please make good use of your time, because you won't get it back."

The conversation I had with this shamed single lady would have gone differently only five years ago. There would have been a long diatribe about her value and the tribal bullying that was causing her to question it. I am 78 percent certain I would have quoted Alice Walker at least once and Audre Lorde into infinity. But with the benefit of those five years of experience, I made the choice to offer this woman my encouragement and not my advice.

Because my life has allowed me the privilege to live, I am allowing others do so as well.

I DON'T KNOW IF UPROOTING MY LIFE WAS THE MAGIC wand that revived it. Sometimes I miss New York City with an intensity that surprises and saddens me. My daily routine follows the same format as it did in my home country. I am in bed by ten. When I want to be grown and sexy, I shave above the knee, put on makeup, and iron a dress. No matter where I end up going for the evening, I am back home by midnight and in REM sleep by 12:17.

I do not sleep in youth hostels when I go on vacation. I do not long for the simplicity of "local" life when I overcome language barriers enough to engage in conversation with a "regular" citizen of the country where I have been allowed to take up residence. I have not been on a transformative spiritual pilgrimage in these foreign lands any more than I was when I began practicing Buddhism in the United States.

All those questions I had three years ago when I began looking for jobs overseas still have not been answered. I have found half-answers that have led to more questions that are worded in similar fashion to the original ones. I shy away from heralding my life as anything other than just that: a life (that I do my best to live with joy). Far too many people throw words such as "courageous," "bold," and "inspiring" at me.

"People who tell me they admire me weird me out," Sabrina has said when we've talked about visiting home. "I just found this job and moved to where it was."

And this is the new predicament in which Sabrina and I

now find ourselves. We have not done anything big, yet we have. We do not have lives different from other women like us, yet we do.

My last three months in Kigali were spent dodging requests from my maid to buy her a house and rushing the gate guard to the emergency room after his wife (allegedly) poisoned him for his (likely) extramarital affairs. Souda's requests for funding for a house could have been just her normal requests for loans. She requested an advance on a portion of her salary several times throughout my two years there, which I gave to her as a gift. But somehow her labored, "There is house . . . sometimes boss help you . . . this house . . . very good house to buy" didn't feel the same as her "daughter sick . . . no medicine." Up until my last bag was packed, I thwarted these inquiries by smiling and looking confused, as if this were the first time she had tried to speak to me in clipped English interspersed with Kinyarwanda.

After only three months in Shanghai, I considered booking a flight to Hong Kong to go on a three-day hunt for birth control pills comparable to the brand I used in the States, booked an actual flight to Malaysia for dental work, and flew to Japan for twenty-four hours to visit the headquarters of the Buddhist organization I have belonged to for the last eight years. My last three Christmases were spent in South Africa, the Seychelles, and Bali, respectively. Whenever I leave my apartment to embark on any errand, I utilize three different apps if I am to achieve any modicum of success.

My friends back home don't have to dodge housekeepers who seek sponsorship on big-ticket items such as homes. They aren't awakened in the middle of the night by the piercing screams of a man near death. They go to the pharmacy for birth control pills and roll their eyes when their dentist increases their copay. They spend the holidays arguing with aunties about who will make the gumbo, and when they go to the grocery store to pick up forgotten ingredients, they do not have to put themselves at the mercy of iTranslate and spotty wifi just to come back to the house with what they thought was milk but is some other white, creamy substance useless for making mac and cheese.

When people seek my advice about their own international move, I am as candid about how much my life has been enriched by leaving the United States as I am cautious not to present the relocation alone as the source of my enrichment. Particularly after the tragedy that occurred the night of the presidential election, the cries to "escape while I can" intensified in tone and volume. Several messages showed up in my social media platforms. *I am very serious about this. How do I move abroad?*

I understood the fear and fatigue. Any person of color who didn't feel it (in the States) or understand it (while living abroad) could be classified as willfully blind. However, I remained as true in my responses to these post-catastrophe inquiries as I had been before: if you plan a move as an escape from something, you are less likely to get the story of adventurous triumph you seek.

There is something to be said for the universality of life. You take yourself with you wherever you go and are tasked with the same struggle in each place you land: how to overcome yourself. I fought that battle waiting for the 6 train at E. 177th Street in the dead of winter. I fought that battle bored out of my mind with the eerie quiet of the lush and beautiful Kigali. I fought that battle in the super city of Shanghai. I am thankful that I never expected this life abroad to save me from myself. If I had, I would be a broken, bitter woman. Living outside of American borders has given me more of myself, which has made me even better equipped for the continued work of self-salvation.

7

———

What the Wound Reveals

*I*f you're not careful, this life will crack you wide open. While you are traveling to the latest country. While you are laughing at the latest miscommunication that resulted in your being in a different place than you thought you told the driver. While you are reveling in all the money that remains in your savings account. If you don't pay attention, your adventurous life laced with privilege will reveal ruptures. Not in your life itself (no, that will still be privileged and awesome), but in you. They will look like tiny abrasions at first—as in, getting off the moto before checking to see if your leg was far enough away from the tailpipe. If you are not paying attention, you will be scooting around your new city with all your insides hanging out, leaving a trail of truths behind for these latest foreigners to assess in a language you do not understand.

I watched connections form in Kigali. So many sets of friends because there was no one else there. So many relationships—from casual hookups to marriages—that began and continued simply because the other person was there.

I remember the first time a colleague brought her boyfriend to a work function. He had been standing by the bar talking to a guy I knew from seeing around the main office. When I walked up to order a glass of wine, I assumed that the guy from the main office had brought along his homeboy as a plus-one.

"Hey, how do you know Pascal?" I asked this new face.

"Through this party," the new face said, laughing. "We were both talking about how we might be retirement age by the time we got our beers and then you came up. That is the entire history of our friendship."

The coworker introduced the new face as the boyfriend of a woman who I had lunch with every single day. A woman who mocked me with a smile whenever my Americanness came out in full force, thus threatening her Britishness. She had mentioned this boyfriend once in one of our many conversations, so I knew she was involved with a local man. A lot of expats were.

But *this* was her local man? Unlike those travel blogs bemoaning all these white women coming into black and brown countries and "buying" themselves eligible-enough single men, my coworker's boyfriend didn't surprise me because it was obvious he had finagled his way into a potential green-card relationship. He veered just as far from the big black buck with all the right moves prototype as much as my coworker strayed quite some ways from the overweight, homely white girl who would not have been able to get a man back in England. I didn't know enough about him or her to draw conclusions about the relationship other than they both professed to being in one. But before I even saw the two of them together, something struck me as "off" about this being the boyfriend she had mentioned. During our conversation at the bar (drawn out in length because I, too, anticipated being able to collect social security right after the bartender brought my drink), I found myself wondering how the two of them had gotten together.

When the British woman joined her boyfriend in another conversation he was having later that evening, I came to the conclusion that they had gotten together because he was there. The way he stood next to her. Her hand hanging at her side and him making no effort to grasp it. The gap between them so wide that no one would discern them as anything other than two random guests at a semi-mandated work function. The way he looked at her and she at him when the group conversation they were involved in broke off into several sets of dialogues before each pair returned to the central conversation. The way they engaged when they were having private moments bared no resemblance to lovers sharing a quick connection before returning back to the world others inhabited. It looked like the conversation the boyfriend had been having with Main Office Guy at the bar, except that conversation had appeared much more natural; I'd mistaken them for friends when I walked up, after all.

"I didn't expect him to be groping his girl in the middle of the Christmas party or for her to start dry humping him in the corner, but seriously, there seemed to be no chemistry between them at all," I told a good friend several days later. We were only talking about the odd coupling because she had been trying to make me feel guilty for not being more welcoming to an acquaintance neither of us liked, but who kept trying to invite herself into our genuine friendship whenever she saw us together. My unapologetic response to her "Now, you know that woman was waiting for you to ask her to sit down" was "But neither of us wanted her to sit down, though."

Even though my real friend had the same initial reaction to the acquaintance as I did—forced smile and polite "Hi, how are you"—she wanted to play the game that I had grown weary of playing shortly after moving to a foreign country. You pretend that because you are in a foreign country, you must somehow shape your personality into a new mold, one that will help you survive in this new country. So, instead of admitting that this nice woman you keep seeing around at events is not that important to you, you try to make yourself believe that she *can* be important to you.

She is there, isn't she? You are there, too, aren't you? So, why not just be there together? Until . . . You are standing next to each other at some function looking like two of the most oddly matched "friends" in the history of agape love.

About four months into my first international post, I realized I was friends with a woman who I did not like very much. She had not done anything cruel to me nor was she a bad person. I just didn't connect with her. And yet here I was, accepting invitations to go places with her, coming up with things for us to do so we could become even closer "friends." Feeling bad for making up excuses for why I had to reschedule those things I did not want to do in the first place. I watched other acquaintances do this too. Expats determined to recreate the social networks they lost once they left their home countries gravitating to other English-speaking foreigners. Or paying off the locals with rounds of beer and sub-sidized trips to neighboring countries because "we are friends and if they could afford to return the favor, they would."

The initial attempt at friendship is innocent enough. You strike up a conversation with someone at work. You are having a cup of coffee and reading a book when the person sitting across from you asks where you are from. Small talk follows.

This is where shit can get weird. You put more burden on the back of this small talk than you ever would have if you were in the Starbucks on 145th Street. This mindless chatter is elevated from "Things People Do When They Are Stuck in Line Together" to "The Universe's Hint This Might Be My New Best Friend." You decide that you have to make more effort. You have to call this new person and invite her out to see that show on Friday night. If you don't say yes to her first invitation to hang out, then you are not taking this new life seriously. You could have just stayed on your sofa in the Bronx watching Netflix. Why'd you move all the way over here if you weren't going to make more effort to expand your horizons?

None of these attempts to widen your life for a new friend are bad. The building of relationships does require a bit of effort and compromising your normal routine. The friends back home who you make as much effort to keep in touch with via Facebook only became your support system because one day many years ago you were at this poetry reading and this woman read a kick-ass poem and you told her after, "Wow, that was exquisite" and then she told you about this writer's retreat she was thinking about applying to and . . . next thing you know, fifteen years later, she is your ace.

And it is that knowledge that propels you into the world of superficial friendships abroad. You do not listen to the voice that whispers, "But there is nothing there on which to base all of this compromise." You choose to only hear, "Just give this woman you are indifferent about a chance. It might be your only one." And if the potential friend is a halfway decent human being—she doesn't treat the waiter like shit, she has good things to say about most people, etc.—then your decision to throw yourself full force into this friendship that does not yet exist will only be further enabled by this determination to make effort. It is a subtle struggle to convince yourself that you are only doing what you did fifteen years ago when you met your dear friend and had no idea when you both signed up for the writer's retreat together you would end up as each other's emergency contact a decade later.

What you underestimate is the time it takes to formulate friendships that matter. Friendships worth biting your tongue until it bleeds because you know the words you are chewing down into paste would destroy the person you love. Friendships worth doing things you don't want to do on days when you could be doing such things for money. Friendships that are worth salvaging. They tend to take more than a few experiences to cultivate. Such bonds don't form by force. Connections don't just happen because you keep trying to make them happen.

TWO MONTHS INTO MY FIRST POST, I DECIDED I NEEDED to have a local friend. It didn't matter who that friend was. It didn't matter if that person were interested in being my friend as much as I was in being hers. I chose a Rwandan woman who was young enough to know where cool things would happen but old enough to value being home by midnight. I targeted the victim of my thirst at work and proceeded to make suggestion after suggestion to a young woman who blew me off with "maybes" and "we will sees" for as long as she possibly could.

"I've never been to Giseyne," I would try to bait her.

"Oh, really," she would respond.

Silence would follow. Instead of waiting for an invitation to explore together, I would suggest that she and some of her friends take me to places I had never been.

"It would be fun! Like a girl's weekend right on Lake Kivu!"

I would pretend that her lack of enthusiasm about this hypothetical weekend was unimportant; I was excited enough for both of us. While my fake friendship with the woman I tolerated was flourishing around this same time, I somehow did not recognize that perhaps I was to this woman what my non-friend was to me.

There are single expats who employ this put-energy-into-a-person-you-don't-really-like strategy in their dating lives too. Shantal, a divorced mother of two, talked to me about going on an awful date with another expat in Kuwait.

The date was average and she felt no chemistry for the man —who, for his part, suggested that their boring date might pick up if they had sex.

For a moment after Shantal arrived home that night, she considered calling her date to see if he had made it back to his place okay. "I wanted to crawl out of my skin and slap myself as soon as the thought came into my head," she told me. (She had received no such "Did you make it home alright?" message from her date, mind you.) She, of course, accepted that this fleeting thought should remain just that and deleted the delusional dude's number from her phone. He had seen the reality of what had transpired more clearly than she had. He had spent two hours of his life with someone who saw no reason to spend two hours and one second more with him. And he did not see the need to force any further interactions because neither one cared enough to make them happen (clothed or otherwise).

In Kigali, I found myself playing this same game with men. I would accept a date from a man who I had observed to be a low-level asshole. I knew he was a secret sexist, yet I chose to believe he was merely a product of his culture. A belief system rooted in strict gender roles did not have to mean a man supported patriarchy, now did it? I would sit through dates where every question this man asked only confirmed that he was, in fact, a sexist asshole. And every response I gave as a woman who did not idolize motherhood or marriage and openly mocked the suggestion that either were the greatest roles I would ever play confirmed I was not the ideal companion for this nice sexist with deep asshole tendencies.

Yet when invitations for other dates popped up in my WhatsApp messages, I put on foundation, ironed a dress, and showed up to have tedious, exhausting conversations with an irritating man. There is a great amount of farce involved in continuing to respond to messages from a man who you did not like when you accepted a date from him and quickly decided on that date was an asshole, and not a very cute one at that. There is a dogged decision to believe you are just trying to be more open.

"Let me give this a chance. Isn't that why I moved? For new experiences."

Much like the lies you tell yourself when you hang out with acquaintances you don't like, the dates with men you do not like shield you from the one emotion that moving abroad brings into super sharp focus.

Loneliness is not an emotion only the international globetrotter feels. It is one that every human will feel at points throughout their life, regardless of who is or is not in that life when the emotion surfaces. There is something that loneliness experienced abroad reveals, though. I have seen it reveal how delusional you can become about *why* you continue to nurture a friendship with a woman when the only common trait shared between you is the ability to speak English. You tell yourself that you are sitting through awkward conversations with this woman who irritates you because you don't want to rush to judgment. She is probably just as in need of friendship as you are. She is just there. That is why you still talk to her.

Just like the average-looking asshole. You are not returning his messages because you are trying to figure out if the assholey things he says are just cultural idiosyncrasies that your Western mind doesn't quite understand. But no, he is an asshole who is just there. And this is why you have not told him, "Stop contacting me." He is there. And his being there offers you comfort if you choose to take it. It offers you an out. If you choose to take it.

What expat loneliness can also reveal is that you are a damn good liar. You could release these people from your life, but the lie you tell yourself is that it is nicer to lead people on, continuing to pretend you are interested in a connection, than to allow them the time to nurture a connection with someone who does value them in ways you do not. You convince yourself the lie is about the fake friend and the asshole dude. It is to spare their hurt feelings. But it is really about you. You would feel bad admitting you are collecting people you don't want to keep.

"Some of these people are going to find themselves stuck by the end of this school year," I told a colleague who was new to this world of international teaching, where it is not unusual for folks to relocate to other countries on other sides of the world every two years.

"They are making friends with coworkers out of convenience." I was referencing the too-eager smiles and too-quick acceptances of every activity suggested. "Once they realize they don't really like each other all that much, they will have pretended for so long it will become almost impossible to back out of the pretense."

The newbie looked away from me, thinking about the friends she was making in this exciting yet frightening new life she had chosen. It wasn't my intent to make my coworker question what could possibly be authentic friendships. But then she nodded her head in the affirmative. "Yup, I know exactly what you mean."

She had only been doing what she thought she should be doing: Giving everyone a chance. Being open. Distracting herself from having to answer that question in her head: *Did you really do the right thing by leaving behind all that was familiar?*

FACING THIS NEW CHALLENGE CAN BECOME TOO MUCH for some. I watched two women in two different countries break a contract after barely finishing a full semester. In Rwanda, the woman's wounds were so wide, the stench of the untreated injuries taking up the whole room, that it was not at all surprising when she said good-bye to the faculty at the Christmas party, stating, "Sometimes, a country is just not a good fit." I nodded my head with everyone else and wished her well in whatever she planned to do next. I recalled a conversation we had had as I was making copies in the teacher's lounge a few weeks before.

"The people here are just . . ."

I waited for her to find the least judgmental way to judge an entire country of people.

"I guess I expected them to be more open, more willing to connect."

The translation of that critique: "Rwandans are indifferent to my presence. This bothers me because I wanted them to give me the authentic African experience."

And for expats who roll into these countries burdening

its countrymen with the responsibility of transforming them, the indifference of the citizens can be quite damaging to their sense of self. I regularly amused myself by watching white expats, particularly, analyze and dissect why none of the local staff made much effort to get to know them. "Why won't they invite me over to their house? I had everyone over after the first week of school." Because they don't care to, perhaps? Because they would rather invest their post-work energy in people they know will be in Kigali longer than two years?

In China, one Boston native left in the middle of the night. I assume she had informed her supervisors in advance and it was only her colleagues who felt like she had been teaching in the morning one day, but then by sixth period had cleared out her desk and thrown away dry erase markers that had another few days of use left in them.

"What? She quit?" the questions began. "I knew she didn't love it here, but I thought she had adjusted enough by now to at least finish out the year."

The whispers were short-lived because we all had seen enough in the countries where we worked to know that sometimes too much change, too many unforeseen variables factored into a new life, can add up to a costly price not worth paying.

Like the British woman who had decided Rwanda was not the right country for her, I reviewed the encounters I'd had with this American woman from the day the human resources staff picked us both up from Pudong Airport. About a week after we had introduced ourselves during our jet-lagged drive to the school's campus, she was bemoaning her boyfriend taking so long to return her phone calls because there was a twelve-hour time difference between them. I said to myself: "Um . . . has it even been two full weeks since you've been in China?" Her need to talk to this man as often as she had when they lived a few miles from each other seemed to speak of a woman who should have never left the man in the first place.

When the boyfriend popped up in Shanghai a month later and stayed for two weeks, I saw her brighten a bit. A smile rested in the curve of her lips and she seemed able to deal with the greasy, salty nature of Shanghainese cuisine. Her scowls were downgraded to frowns when she had to take out her wet wipes to clean a dirty fork in a restaurant or when a local man sneezed, hacked up spit, or coughed without bothering to cover his mouth.

But when, at the beginning of the third week, the boyfriend went back to Boston, he took his girlfriend's lessened misery with him. I was not close friends with her, but we did have occasional conversations about our adjustment to Shanghai. She was in her late twenties, and I knew living so far away from downtown city life had to be difficult for her. She was still young enough to have an active night life without being mocked as the old lady in the club, yet she lived in this sprawling suburb an hour away from civilization on a gated boarding school campus that had no interaction with anyone or anything outside its gates. She was in an isolated bubble within an isolated bubble.

Our first long break came in October. She was on a plane back to her boyfriend before the final school bell had rung. For the Christmas holiday, she and the boyfriend met up in Mexico. While she was making friends with other teachers and did come out to group gatherings, it was clear that she had underestimated how much quality face-to-face time with the man she loved was integral to her happiness. So, yes, by the time Chinese New Year was upon us, that Yankee had had enough. *I gave it a shot*, I am sure she thought as she threw her clothes in a suitcase, not bothering to pack up the few trinkets she had bought in the last five months.

When I think about these two expats who didn't make it, their different reasons for leaving their posts stem from the same problem: inability to connect in an authentic way with another human being in their new surroundings. In the case of my colleague in Rwanda, she had tried to engage but had discovered it would take time and extra effort to garner the trust of the people she'd just met. For Westerners who believe themselves worthy of the praise and adulation of everyone in the world, doing such interpersonal work can seem daunting and unfair. So, some of us just opt out.

In the case of the colleague in Shanghai, she didn't truly understand what moving thousands of miles away meant for her relationship. There are many expats who have left significant others in their home countries and from what I have observed, these long-distance relationships can and do work under the right circumstances. However, the partner that now lives in another part of the world will not make her adjustment smoother by making no effort to build community and connection in her new home, no matter how temporary the home. One woman could have found herself in a fake friendship that disillusioned her to a problematic new life. The other had decided she needed neither fake nor real friends. She had a man many miles away.

⌒

THE FAKE FRIEND I NEVER QUITE BROKE UP WITH IN Kigali stayed in my circle the entire two years I was there. Kigali is a tiny place where you will walk into any establishment for any event in any part of town and run into at least four different people from four aspects of your life. So there was no way to be social without seeing her and having to make nice. The week before I was to leave, I thought about her. How relieved I was I would not have to pretend anymore, having to avoid voicing my real feelings about her in mixed company as well as trying to be civil with her without leading her on to believe I really wanted friendship from her.

I vowed to never do that again. When I taught at a secondary school in New York City, I had mediation sessions with girls who were not friends and never should have pretended they were. For adolescent girls, finding the balance between "being nice" and "being authentic" is made more difficult by a culture that encourages the female person to sacrifice all for the sake of saving others' feelings. I remember having an advisory discussion about why lying to someone about wanting to be their friend was just as cruel as bullying a weaker student or staying silent while someone else was doing the bullying.

"But, how do you say that—'I don't want to be your friend'—without sounding really mean?" one of my advisees asked me.

I didn't have an answer then. Two years with my fake friend provided me with a possible answer years later, however.

You don't need to say, "I don't want to be your friend."
You just need to be honest in your initial interactions with a
new person so they know where they stand. You treat people
you don't know with kindness and respect without jumping
into friendships that cannot exist because you have not determined who they are to the extent that you can call yourselves more than acquaintances.

IMMEDIATELY UPON ARRIVING IN SHANGHAI, I WATCHED
one lonely person after another realize they were alone. Their
eyes gave them away. Their "Sure, I'll go with you!" eagerness
was a telltale sign that they were afraid if they did not attach
themselves to another human being as soon as possible, they
would be doomed to themselves in this big, scary city for the
next two years.

Several of them tried to attach themselves to me. "I just
came up to see what you were doing," Tabitha, another faculty
member who lived on campus, would say to me when she
showed up at my door. She had gotten in the habit of stop-
ping by my apartment unannounced, carrying baked goods as
bribes. I had met this woman less than thirty days earlier and
yet she was stepping over lines that I assumed most adults
did not need explicitly drawn once they had passed the age of
twenty-one.

I smiled as she stood at my door, waiting for me to invite
her in. "Oh, you've been baking again, I see," I said. She offered me a freshly baked cookie, which I knew came with
conditions. *Since you don't want to be my friend just because I
want you to be my friend, perhaps you will like me because I can*

bake! This was the third time she had found herself at my home at the same time I was. The second time, too, she had offered me a cookie to convince me to erase the line I would have been more willing to ignore had she been less determined to force friendship on me.

I thanked her for thinking of me while making it clear I wanted to spend my evening alone.

Since Kigali, I had established some ground rules. Group activities with colleagues only. Most schools organize welcome dinners and city tours for new teachers before the school year begins. I had gone to these activities and enjoyed the camaraderie and shared stories of previous posts in parts of the world that interested me. If I did not find myself intrigued with any of the people there, I found a reason not to spend extra time with them alone.

I briefly struggled with how this polite avoidance would be perceived. I am a funny and easy-going person, which often draws people to me. Also, I extend sincere compassion to every human being with whom I come into contact. What would a woman make of my asking after her well-being but still not trying to become her real friend?

Luckily, I had released myself from responsibility for others' reaction to me and the manner in which I decided to navigate my world years ago. This made it easier to be okay with showing compassion to people I would not ever call true friends.

Women who struck me as incomplete and clingy would not get a private friendship date with me. I would put their names on my altar and chant for their happiness, but I would not invite them into my life. I had decided there were certain flaws in people that I could accept as their own fallibility and at the same time work doggedly to keep such imperfection out of my environment.

Jennifer, another Shanghai colleague, shared with a table of eight strangers that every man she has ever dated has been in prison.

"I don't know how it happens," she said, launching into the most TMI of all such stories a person could tell. "But we'll be together for like three months and then when I ask the guy why he's having problems finding another job, he will say, 'Well, I should have told you this before . . .'"

Jennifer seemed blind to the looks of discomfort that followed her story. She continued with stories of boyfriends who had stolen from her, and even a boyfriend who had exploded in rage when she suggested he would have better success at starting his own business if he took an actual course at the local community college.

I recognized Jennifer's nonstop oversharing at a school-sponsored happy hour for what it was. A woman who had left the United States because she believed the country was the problem and was getting started on this "new life" in China by being self-deprecating in front of potential friends. She was hoping maybe some of the other single girls around the table would see themselves in her and want to swap stories of self-induced trauma over cocktails later. I chuckled and walked away as Jennifer asked for the second time since I'd met her, "Wanna add me on Facebook?" By the third request (which came about three days later), I decided to add a direct answer: "We have each other's information on WeChat. That should be enough."

NO THANKS | 149

Men who I could not even imagine taking off my bra for in the United States of America would not be having anything more than casual conversation with me in China. It did not matter that cultural differences caused a divide between us. I was unconcerned that my progressive, feminist views would go unchallenged—thus locking me into a biased view of love and partnership—by not breaking bread with foreign or local Neanderthals who wanted to offer me the nice consolation prizes of patriarchy. None of the unpleasantness.

My requirement for real friendship is much simpler than the ground rules I have outlined. Upon encountering someone—male or female, countryman or expat from elsewhere, local or longtime foreigner—I ask myself this question: If I were still living in New York City, if I were able to speak the language fluently and communicate with most people here, if I were not afraid of being in this strange country alone, would I still want to spend time with this person? If the answer is a firm yes, then let's put gas in the car, check the brakes, and embark on this spectacular journey to friendship! Anything other than a firm yes is a solid no and the beginning of a tiresome trek into an abysmal lie.

AS I CONTINUED THIS POLITE DISTANCE FROM PEOPLE at my post in Shanghai, I watched as alliances formed. Some seemed to be authentic bonds that would survive contract renewal when one or both friends would move on to their next post. Others struck me as the beginning of two years of awkward interactions that neither would know how to extricate themselves from the longer they allowed the charade to continue.

I do not begrudge these people their superficial friendships. There is an element to expat life that is hard to explain. The best I have been able to do is to compare it to a freshman who chooses to attend an out-of-state college. Leaving home is a requisite part of American adulthood, but most of your peers would have done it closer to the home they were leaving. When I was going away to college, the farthest anyone in my peer group went was Baton Rouge, a forty-five-minute drive from New Orleans. I thought I was doing big things by "going away" to live in the dorm of the University of New Orleans.

If you amplify this analogy and apply it to moving abroad as a full-fledged adult, consider this: Even fewer peers leave the country for a vacation, let alone a relocation. And unless your relocation is to a country similar in culture and customs to the United States, you are guaranteed all of those "I can't wait to visit" promises will be empty ones. I had a girlfriend flat-out tell me, "When you make it back to North America—like maybe if you find a job in Costa Rica—I will holla at ya."

Also, I would be remiss if I did not mention that the reason why you would have chosen a country different from the United States is the same reason why you will find yourself frustrated as you try to adjust to how laws work in a government that is not democratic and how people behave when they are indifferent to how you expect them to behave.

The same way you ended up naked in that stupid boy's dorm room in the middle of the night and at the dining hall table with that mean, gossipy girl is how you end up breaking bread with sexist assholes and pretending to be friends with petty women who never have anything interesting to talk about.

If you are an adult who has paid attention to who you are and what you want—if you have worked to form some connection to a spiritual core—you will be better prepared for your new life than you were when you were a teenager who had no idea how much you did not know.

It's the expats whose only preparation for an international move was stocking up on their favorite junk food who are often the first to throw themselves at strangers, seeking friendship the way loose girls seek dates. They have done little spiritual work and even less reflection on their motivations and desires. These people get off the plane in their new homes and run straight for the delusions that plagued them in their old ones. A boyfriend Band-Aid or frenemy façade are predictable accessories for a person who does not feel safe and is not ready to admit it.

It is not just those of us who move abroad alone who apply weak salve to our wounds. Tabitha baked so often because her teenaged son and husband of twenty years loved her desserts. In her continued attempts to corner me into friendship, I felt more sympathy for her than I did for Jennifer. Something about her deep sense of isolation felt much sadder than Jennifer's willingness to humiliate herself in front of strangers on the slim chance that one of them would use her for more entertaining anecdotes when they, too, were lonely and bored.

If I were still into the whole lying because I am trying to

be "new" in a foreign country thing, I would have collected Jennifer and Tabitha for as long I needed them. I would have given them the sense of safety my insincere friendship would have provided. The unfortunate truth, though, is that none of us would have been any safer than we would have been when we stopped lying. We would have to face the reality of what we had done. We had left our families. We had left our friends. We had left our good jobs. We had left all the distractions those families and friends and good jobs provided.

The rush to find replacements for those distractions would be the catalyst for being cracked open more so than it would be the magic elixir to stop it from happening in the first place.

8

Letting the Loose Woman Remain Free

*O*f I could write her a letter, it would be short and sweet: Dear Ava, please don't do to Nova Bordelon what *The Cosby Show* did to Denise Huxtable. Please *do not* Whitley Gilbert her, either.

I loved both shows then and still value them now. Were it not for *The Cosby Show* I would have had no reason to remember it was Thursday night, and *A Different World* made me even more impatient to become an adult and go away to college. I am sure there is not one episode of either show that I have not seen at least twice. For all my love and appreciation for documentation of black life not rooted in suffering, however, there is still a sour taste in my mouth about the trope both shows played into: turning free black women into tamed caretakers.

It started with Denise. She was the wild Huxtable child. She had flunked out of Hillman and was floundering around with no direction, so she was sent to Africa to do field work with (presumably) an anthropologist. Her curiosity about life, coupled with a potential that formal schooling had failed to nurture, convinced Cliff and Claire that perhaps this year-long exploration of the world outside of Brooklyn Heights would be good for her.

She came back from Africa with a husband and step-daughter. In the seasons that followed, she doted over little Olivia and got into minor skirmishes with Martin as they tried to create a married life while living in her parents' home.

There are worse things the writers could have done to Denise, I suppose. She could have died in the bush. She could have come back still having no direction or purpose. They chose to "settle" her with a husband and child. If we were not clear that this is exactly what taking on domestic life does for her, a few seasons after she comes home, she decides to pursue a career in education and returns to the local university. Being a mother has matured her, you see. Having a successful husband who wants to start a home of his own has influenced her in a positive way.

We should applaud this.

When Dwayne Wayne interrupted Whitley and Byron's wedding to confess his love for the bourgeois bride everyone liked to mock, Black America collectively had a massive heart attack. There were cheers. There were phone calls from friends who wanted the high-pitched screams on the other end of the line to confirm what they had just seen really did happen. Finally! These two star-crossed lovers had been brought together by Dwayne's "Baby, please." On the hierarchy of grand romantic gestures in '90s black love stories,

Dwayne stealing Whitley from Byron on their wedding day ranks somewhere in between Monica asking Quincy for one more free throw to win back his heart and Darius blazing through those Chicago streets on the back of his motorcycle trying to get to the train station before Nina leaves for New York.

Everyone I knew was talking about the wedding episode for weeks after it aired. Everyone agreed Whitley had shown courage. She had chosen to follow her heart, angering her mother and humiliating her fiancé by running off with her college sweetheart.

The first episode of the next season, however, Whitley had been tamed. As a late teen, I could not identify why my interest in the last season began to wane within the first five minutes of the "Whitley as Struggling Housewife" episode. While she had never been my favorite character on the show, I had understood her to be an opinionated, strong-willed, uppity chick who had always wanted a husband but still wanted other things as well. Still had interesting contributions to make in conversation. A personality as powerful and vibrant as Kimberly's or Jahleesa's.

The writers did not waste time turning Whitley into a tragic victim of domesticity. When I reflect on its expedience, I become agitated. The woman who had just last season been entrusted to run someone's political campaign while still in her twenties was now wringing her hands over failed attempts to make her mother-in-law's prune cobbler. She worried about running the household, had breakdowns over unfolded laundry, and burned dinner. Dwayne, the man we had been led to believe was her soul mate, "supported" her by telling her it was okay if she could not make the prune cobbler now. She was trying and that was all that mattered. She did not have to be his perfect wife right now. It would come with time.

Black love at its finest.

Since Ava Duvernay is a storytelling genius and a free black woman herself, I am confident I do not have to appeal to her to allow Nova Bordelon to remain free. I trust her to write Nova into a woman who has love and herself at the same time. I know she is an intentional filmmaker and nothing that happens to Nova occurs as an afterthought. Her story, her character, her struggles have been crafted with care. Nova has been sculpted under the knowing eye of a woman who is probably just as irritated as I am about what those writers did to Denise and Whitley.

There have already been signs that I can trust Ava with a character that can so easily be drawn with the harsh brush of cynicism. I suspect I will not tune in to *Queen Sugar* every week, holding my breath as I hope that Nova will still be allowed to choose herself. Nova has already done the unthinkable: she has turned down a good black man. She has given no reason for doing so other than she did not believe this good black man would support the parts of her that she valued the most. She rejected the opportunity to partner with an intellectual and spiritual equal because she was not confident he respected the life she saw for herself and was offended by his bold suggestion that he knew of a better way for her to be Nova. It should be noted that unlike Denise and Whitley, Nova is a seasoned, accomplished woman well into her thirties. She is not a late adolescent who has not yet had enough experiences to confidently proclaim: THIS IS WHO I AM. Nova is a woman who has lived, loved, failed, and succeeded in her womanhood for almost two decades. Yet it appears that even she can be viewed as wet cement begging for her lover's imprint.

Nova Bordelon's relationship with Dr. Robert Dubois begins with her hesitancy from their first flirtatious exchange. Since she is a journalist committed to racial justice in New Orleans's culturally rich Lower Ninth Ward, Robert's work as an academic and commitment to using the resources provided by academia to fund black empowerment projects draws her to him. But she has doubts about their compatibility from the moment they decide to become "official." Some of those doubts are rooted in how Robert goes about funding racial justice projects. He is not above playing nice with racists in order to bilk them of their money. He admits to Nova that he panders to white colleagues whom he knows can be manipulated into donating money to black causes they do not believe worthy of their altruism. This does not sit well with Nova, ideological purist that she is. Yet she continues the courtship anyway.

After allowing Robert to influence her into making choices that she believes have compromised her values, Nova allows him to share his vision for how her work should continue. The vision is not only incongruent with who Nova is and what she cherishes, the tone in his voice as he outlines what should be her career trajectory is so rich with condescension, I find it baffling that Nova does not cuss him out. Instead she tells him he is a very good man but "you are not good for me."

When Robert sees his imminent dismissal on the horizon, he tries to clean up the damage his attempts to mold this grown woman had done. He asks Nova not to end their relationship. He tells her he loves her and requests a chance to discuss the problems they are having. "We can fix this," he pleads.

Ms. Bordelon is already done.

From the moment Robert confided in Nova that he did not have children because he did not believe they would be a better legacy than the work he was doing for his community, I wanted Nova to give her heart fully to him. I believed Robert was the better choice for long-term partnership than the others Nova had been involved with in these two seasons. Yet I shed a tear of joy when she told this good black man, "I do not need you to dream for me." I launched into a praise twerk in my living room when she cut him off in the middle of his fantasy about the two of them and said, "I should not have to disappear into you to make our relationship work."

Whitley can obsess over prune cobbler, but Nova will not.

Denise needed a child to focus her. A strong marriage to motivate her. Nova does not.

Nova's commitment to self is not the only reason she doesn't even allow Robert a chance to correct his error. The argument has been made that Nova's fear of complete surrender and her unresolved feelings for the man that came before Dubois are just as much an impediment to progress in their relationship as Robert's presumptuous attempt to parent a woman who does not need to be parented. The fans who have made this argument have had an easy enough time proving their case because where Ava's precise pen leaves off, Rutina Wesley's brilliant performance takes over. With a depth and beauty I have never seen captured in media, Rutina keeps giving us a black woman who can be two things at once: courageous warrior and cowardly lion, self-possessed and uncertain, committed to values and hypocritical when those values become inconvenient.

After Nova dismisses Dubois, the one that came before him shows up. There is a brief chance for them to reunite. When Nova sends this man on his way too, Rutina's portrayal of the difficulty in doing so leaves me breathless. Nova feels he stands in the way of her being who she truly is and doing her life's work with full support from her partner.

When Nova turned down Calvin, the white cop who had left his wife for her, right after turning down the black intellectual who had bought her a string of pearls, the internet lost its mind.

"I don't get it. They both were fine and had good jobs."

"She is confused."

"She does not appreciate a good man."

"She does not know what love is."

"She is going to end up alone, full of regrets."

I knew I needed to see Nova from the very first episode. I did not know the world needed to see her, too, until I joined the *Queen Sugar* discussion group on Facebook. When Nova dismissed two men in back-to-back episodes, Black America was angry in a way that struck me as having nothing to do with why they said they were angry.

Nova had not been cruel to either of these men. She realized she did not want to continue further with them and told them so. She acknowledged to them and to herself that this was her interpretation of how the relationship was going. Admitted her desire for something else was fueling her need to break things off. Not once did she accuse them of being anything other than decent men who were not what she needed right now.

Yet she was viewed as confused. When reminded of the eloquent explanations she gave both men about why she was leaving, fans still insisted, "She doesn't know what she wants."

People felt sorry for her because they concluded no man had ever loved her like the good black one she had rejected, which was why she did not know how to handle him. It was pointed out that Calvin had not only left his wife to prove he was serious about being with her, he had risked his job by going behind the scenes to get a teenaged black boy she was mentoring released from jail. Every attempt Nova had made on her own had resulted in that young man's fate becoming bleaker.

"She has never been loved," the concerned fans insisted.

By the time members of the discussion group began calling her a ho who was not interested in anything other than sex, I had figured out why this woman and her choices irritated black folk so. Not only did they not believe that Novas existed in real life, they did not believe that Novas had the *right* to exist in real life.

It is the reason why Denise Huxtable had to be put into a marriage with a child in order for us to see a girl mature into a woman. It is why Whitley Gilbert had to spend her first few months as a new wife trying to fix her husband the perfect dessert instead of working on a business plan for her own art gallery—a passion she had talked about several times throughout the show's run.

There is nothing more egregious than a black woman deciding that she will not care for a good man. Particularly a good black one. There is nothing more incomprehensible than a woman supplying flimsy excuses like, "You are my prison" for allowing a man who loves her to walk out the door.

BEFORE NOVA SAYS NO TO LOVE, SHE STEALS THOUSANDS of dollars from her sister. Their father has left his farm to her and her two siblings. The farm has been in their family for generations and the father fought off racists and droughts to keep it in the family. Charley, the most financially secure of the siblings, has contributed her money to an account that the three have agreed will be used for maintenance of the farm. When Nova is trying to get the young man she is mentoring out of jail, "borrowing" money from that account for legal fees is the only thing she can come up with. She does not bother clearing this with her siblings, nor does she ever replace the money she has taken, as she promises she will.

Nova exaggerates a health crisis in the Lower Ninth Ward because it will bring media attention and money for rebuilding the area that still struggles over a decade after Hurricane Katrina. It is Robert's idea for her to fabricate the potential threat of the Zika virus in the Lower Nine and she feels uncomfortable with it, but she does it anyway. The move instills an irrational fear in the residents of that community and plants seeds of doubt among those residents about her credibility as a journalist and activist. Just as she feared.

Yet it is her rejection of the good black man that prompted viewers to post, "I am done with Nova"; "She is exhausting and frustrating."

She explained to Calvin that she could not get back with him because of his willful blindness to the corruption in the police department. She could not overlook his disinterest in how such corruption impacted black people beyond learning just enough to pacify her. At this viewers decried, "This woman is a hypocrite"; "So now she doesn't want the cop either?"

There was no reason she could have given that would have been good enough. No defense to justify why she couldn't just work it out with either of these men. Compromise. Give in just a little. In short: Who the hell does this woman think she is? She keeps getting chosen, but does not seem appreciative of being someone's choice.

I was not surprised when the jokes about her promiscuity found their way into the Facebook threads. It did not take long for viewers to point out how often Nova "opened up her legs." And of course a woman who has sex whenever and with whomever she pleases can never appreciate or even understand a real relationship. She does not deserve one with a good man in the first place.

In short: Who the hell does this Nova heffa think she is to be offered the prize that only black women who behave properly should get and then dismiss that prize as if she were entitled to it in the first place?

There is a scene from *The Cosby Show* that I used to consider benign but I now find disturbing. Cliff decides he needs to get to know his new son-in-law better, so he and Martin spend the day bonding. The two are sitting in the kitchen

discussing how Denise and Martin met. When Martin re-
calls their courtship and smiles about how quickly they fell in
love, Cliff starts poking around with subtle questions about
their sex life. He insinuates that he hopes his daughter was a
virgin when the two "got together." If that isn't bizarre
enough, instead of calling Cliff creepy and getting up from
the table, Martin grins and confirms that yes, he was Denise's
first and only. The two men then beam with pride.

While there were no slutty women as a regular part of
the cast on *A Different World*, the show did tackle the politics
of sex in its own twentieth-century way. Kimberly Reese had
a pregnancy scare once. Freddie was crazy glued to her
boyfriend's body whenever the two appeared together in any
scene, so we all pretty much assumed that they were on their
way to having sex or had just gotten busy right before walking into The Pit. Jahleesa had an ex-husband; she dated
Walter and then married Colonel Taylor. Like Jahleesa, these
two men were older than the other coeds, so she was having
respectable, grown-folk sex. Whitley, however, was always
depicted as the consummate good girl: *if* she had sex, it was
only with super-serious boyfriends who got the prize of her
panties after spending months proving they wanted more
than just her panties.

Whitley and Denise were women who had earned the
reward of serious love from serious-minded men. Nova had
not. The "hos don't get chose" mantra did not begin in the
1990s, of course, so it would be unfair to critique these shows
for the antiquated narrative they perpetuated. The narrative
that suggests a woman's sexuality does not exist merely for
her pleasure, it is also a bartering tool in negotiations for

committed partnership. Nova mounting men and women and enjoying the pleasures of the flesh with no consideration about how this might impact her ability to negotiate for a relationship is more maddening than her saying, "No, thanks," when she does get chose.

Nova is supposed to be rode hard and put up wet. Lovers are supposed to only show up at her door in the middle of the night with condoms and half-truths. Yet the good black man shows up at the airport to collect her holding a placard that reads "QUEEN." The married one gets on his knees and says, "I will do whatever you say I need to do." In between both men, the one she slept with only to get her rocks off with no strings attached tries to attach strings and asks for a real date. The good black woman she courted before the good black man still looks at her as if she is waiting for an invitation back into her life.

Nova Bordelon is everything that black women are not supposed to be if they ever want to win the prize of partnership. It throws people off when this antithesis of the good black womanhood we have come to revere does not seem remorseful for her behavior. Here she is, behaving in ways that are the sole reason why a growing number of good black men have no choice but to wife up white women. Somehow, through forces unexplained, she finds one who is willing to deal with her dogged commitment to self. He doesn't just zip up his pants and drive off after she lures him into the back of his car and says, "I want you now." He actually depletes his frequent flier miles, showing up unannounced on her doorstep. Yet she does not show gratitude for fate granting her favor. She does not thank this man for choosing her by bending herself more to make their relationship work. She chooses singleness when respectable heterosexual partnership is within reach of her slutty arms.

With Nova Bordelon, Ava Duvernay has recreated Sula Peace. Toni Morrison's Sula, a free black woman in 1930s rural America, is a cautionary tale for the good black women of the tiny Ohio town nicknamed "The Bottom." She serves as their measuring stick for how far they can fall into their own freedom without becoming a complete Sula themselves. This woman who takes in men (sometimes, *their* men) and does not have the courtesy to contort herself in the ways they have always done to keep them. Sula, who worships at the altar of herself. So much so that she sends her grandmother off to a nursing home when presented with the noble duty of caring for her. Sula, who on her deathbed still shows no remorse for what a lifetime of freedom has cost those who love her. Her best friend, Nel, begs her to repent of her sin of not birthing and caring for children. Sula will not. Nel also tries to help her friend seek redemption for flouting the role of devoted caretaker of a good man.

"But some men are worth keeping," Nel chastises her.

"Not more than they are worth keeping myself," a dying Sula corrects her friend.

Decades after Morrison showed us what this type of woman looks like, Duvernay and Wesley are taking this antithesis of black womanhood further. They are being honest in their characterization of the impossible battle Nova will always fight because, like her literary predecessor, she is enough for her.

To say "I am enough for me" is not to claim you are

above love and partnership. Wesley does a superb job showing us that Nova does experience loneliness, as all humans
do. It is just not an emotion that so overwhelms her she is
willing to twist herself into more manageable shapes for the
possibility of never feeling it again. She is not dismissive of
love. She just does not value it over any other aspect of her
life. When she tells the cop they will not reconcile, she is at
her most conflicted. Her heart wants what it wants, but she
fears that in order to get what her heart wants she will have
to hide parts of herself. When you are enough for you, there
will never be a man good enough to convince you such a sacrifice is worth it.

In my letter to Ava, I would also say thank you. I know
Novas are better suited for the screen than they are for real
life. To be so rigid in ideology and quick to assume the surrender required in partnership will equate to your erasure will
only result in needless suffering. But fiction is fiction for a
reason. If we can have Denise and Whitley, we can have
Nova. I venture to say we have become too comfortable
watching the Denises and Whitleys make themselves more
manageable. Ava has faith in us: we can handle watching
Nova.

If we are going to amplify black women and their relationship to relationships, I am much more interested in the
Nova extreme. A black woman who at her core operates from
a place of self-preservation. A black woman unwilling to
bend. A black woman who does not desire love more than
she desires herself.

Yes, I'd rather witness that woman on her journey for
forty-five minutes each week.

Acknowledgments

———

Many women were generous with their time throughout this project. I talked with women I believe to be experts in their fields and scholars in their own right—Dr. Kinitra Brooks, Kimberly Peeler-Ringer, Dr. Annalise Fonza, Dr. Kimya N. Dennis, Kimberly Veal, and Jamila Bey, just to name a few. Not only did their insights give me concrete information on which to attach my personal observations, they also challenged my thinking and engaged me in some of the most intellectually rigorous conversations I have had since I was a graduate student.

And then there are my friends. The women who appear here in composites of conversations shared over the years. Women who I called from the other side of the world to ask, "Can we talk about this thing I am writing?" Tracy Adams, Saleeta Spencer-Thomas, Mashadi Mathabane, Courtney Fenner, Ebony Murphy-Root, Donnalee Donaldson, Pamela Dusu and Nicole Whitley are just a few sisterfriends who did not realize how much their perspectives and life choices would make it into this book. While you do not appear by name, I am sure you can spot yourselves quite easily within these pages. We are united by more than our love for Idris and worship of Auntie Toni.

Of course, there are Karen Celestan, Elisabeth Kauffman and Krissa Lagos, who edited out all my overuse of adverbs and oddly constructed sentences. (One day I hope to master this "word economy" thing editors talk so much about.) The production team at She Writes Press and its entire staff have also been instrumental in this book's completion. I thank you all.

About the Author

A New Orleanian by birth and New Yorker by choice, Keturah Kendrick has been penning insights about life at the intersection of race and gender for a decade. Aside from her popular blog, *Yet Another Single Gal*, she has written for *The Unfit Christian*, *The Not Mom*, *NonParents*, and numerous publications. A practicing Nichiren Buddhist and secular humanist, Kendrick seeks to widen the narrative of good black womanhood. Much of her work normalizes and celebrates the black woman who exists outside of the beloved box of gleeful sufferer of fools who sacrifices self for the greater good. She has lived on three different continents and visited dozens of countries. Her travels across the globe have shown her that patriarchy and the worship of whiteness are worldwide illnesses. She should have written *No Thanks* years ago. It is long overdue.

SELECTED TITLES FROM SHE WRITES PRESS

She Writes Press is an independent publishing company
founded to serve women writers everywhere.
Visit us at www.shewritespress.com.

*Stop Giving it Away: How to Stop Self-Sacrificing and Start Claiming
Your Space, Power, and Happiness* by Cherilynn Veland. $16.95, 978-
1-63152-958-0. An empowering guide designed to help women
break free from the trappings of the needs, wants, and whims of
other people—and the self-imposed limitations that are keeping
them from happiness.

(R)evolution: The Girls Write Now 2016 Anthology by Girls Write
Now. $19.95, 978-1-63152-083-9. The next installment in Girls
Write Now's award-winning anthology series: a stunning collection
of poetry and prose written by young women and their mentors in
exploration of the theme of "Revolution."

Love Her, Love Her Not: The Hillary Paradox edited by Joanne
Bamberger. $16.95, 978-1-63152-806-4. A collection of personal
essays by noted women essayists and emerging women writers that
explores the question of why Americans have a love/hate "relationship" with Hillary Clinton.

Dumped: Stories of Women Unfriending Women edited by Nina Gaby.
$16.95, 978-1-63152-954-2. Candid, relatable stories by estab-
lished and emerging women writers about being discarded by
someone from whom they expected more: a close female friend.

*This Way Up: Seven Tools for Unleashing Your Creative Self and
Transforming Your Life* by Patti Clark. $16.95, 978-1-63152-028-0.
A story of healing for women who yearn to lead a fuller life, ac-
companied by a workbook designed to help readers work through
personal challenges, discover new inspiration, and harness their
creative power.

Think Better. Live Better. 5 Steps to Create the Life You Deserve by
Francine Huss. $16.95, 978-1-938314-66-7. With the help of this
guide, readers will learn to cultivate more creative thoughts, realign
their mindset, and gain a new perspective on life.